Good Food No Fuss

Anne Willan

Good Food
No Fuss

Over 150 recipes and ideas
for easy-to-cook dishes

Anne Willan would like to thank:
Kate Rowe, editorial and research associate. Randall Price,
kitchen director. Jessica Battilana, Tamie Cook and Monica
Hulshizer in the test kitchen.

Special photography by Simon Wheeler

Published by BBC Worldwide Limited,
Woodlands, 80 Wood Lane,
London W12 0TT

First published 2003
Text copyright © Anne Willan Inc. 2003
The moral right of the author has been asserted. 34 recipes
have previously appeared in *BBC Good Food Magazine*

Additional photography by Marie Louise-Avery (page 117);
Roger Stowell (pages 7, 26, 43, 46, 56, 78, 120, 126, 132,
133, 145, 151, 157, 158) and Philip Webb (pages 12, 24, 124).
All photographs copyright © BBC Worldwide

ISBN 0 563 48816 6

Commissioning Editor: Vivien Bowler
Project Editor: Vicki Vrint
Consultant Editor: Lewis Esson
Copy Editor: Deborah Savage
Design Manager: Sarah Ponder
Designer: Lisa Pettibone
Food Stylist: Mary Cadogan assisted by Harriet Eastwood
Stylist: Antonia Gaunt
Production Controller: Kenneth McKay

Set in Univers and Minion
Printed and bound in Singapore by Tien Wah Press
Colour separations by Radstock Reproductions

Page 2: *Steak Marchand de Vin* (recipe, page 20)
Page 4–5: *Almond and Cape Gooseberry Torte* (recipe, page 140)
Page 7: *Salmon in Red-wine Sauce* (recipe, page 112)

Contents

Introduction

How I hate a fuss in the kitchen. Too many ingredients, too much work, and worst of all too much washing up. This book is all about simple recipes and easy ways of cooking fresh ingredients. Many dishes take less than half an hour from start to finish, and I promise you many of the ingredients will come from your cupboard. A single pot suffices for recipes such as *Bulgarian Lamb and Vegetable Stew*, or *Portuguese Pork with Clams*. There's even a chapter that involves no cooking at all.

This is the way I cook at home, and it's never dull. So many different ingredients are available now, even in the quiet corner of Burgundy where we live. I'm not looking out for grand cuisine, but for offbeat seasonings and attractive combinations on the plate. Desserts excepted, many of my recipes here are a complete meal, and where an accompaniment is needed, I'm offering suggestions in 'On the Side'. 'In the Glass' talks about wines, beer, and other drinks as well. And as I'm a great proponent of 'Getting Ahead', you'll find advice on this too.

Cooking takes me to many parts of the world, and this book is full of the places I've been and the food I've enjoyed, from Indian curry to Asian stir fries and the splendid soups that warm the Russian winter. It is thanks to our son Simon, resident in Moscow for much of the last dozen years, that I have authentic recipes for soups such as *shchi* (cabbage). Our daughter Emma, a convert to California, has contributed among other treats a delicious pear and fennel salad topped with shavings of Parmesan.

In Burgundy we welcome a multitude of friends and students at La Varenne Cooking School. From them come all kinds of ideas. Chef Randall Price, an American from Ohio, is with us for much of the year and his insights have guided this book. It is thanks to Randall that we've enjoyed dishes like a lusciously creamy pumpkin flan, and thanks to his help in testing that I can assure you that my recipes really do turn out right. As for Kate Rowe, her diligence in editing text and her tact in rewriting recipes have been invaluable.

So please come into the kitchen and call in your friends – it's a great place to start a party!

ANNE WILLAN
www.lavarenne.com

Thirty minutes in the kitchen. It doesn't sound long, but I'm always surprised how much I can accomplish if I really try. There's ample time to bake or fry a piece of fish, for instance, or to bake an egg or whisk up an omelette. On the face of it, meat takes longer, unless served rare as steak, but pork medallions cook quickly too. Chicken breasts could be a problem, but even they can make the time limit if split or sliced. And while these main dishes are on the stove, I can boil potatoes, pasta and most green vegetables as accompaniments.

Once I'm in the kitchen, I have a clear routine: apron on, knives out, and then I line up ingredients on the counter. If something is missing I look for a substitute – shallot for onion, for example, or cinnamon for allspice. Then I put a large pot of salted water to boil and light the oven in anticipation, as both take time to heat. I find I have to break my habit of first preparing ingredients and then cooking them. Given only 30 minutes, the slower-cooking items must start at once – chicken legs must be sautéing, or couscous must already be soaking, while I chop the vegetables that will flavour them.

It is the prep work that takes time, the trimming, peeling and chopping of background ingredients like tomatoes and garlic. Reluctantly, when I'm in a rush I find I can use only a few in each recipe. On the other hand, dried spices and seasonings such as Tabasco and soy sauce are a blessing, though I refuse to compromise by using insipid dried herbs (bay leaf is about the only exception). Don't forget a splash of wine or spirits – surely there's a bottle of something open in the kitchen to pick up a quick little sauce!

Over the years I've collected a handy list of 30-minute standbys, most of them substantial dishes that will anchor a whole meal if I add a simple accompaniment. Many of my recipes have an international flavour – *Roast Cod with Tropical Fruit Salsa* and *Taiwanese Chicken Stir Fry* are typical. Most importantly, I like lively food that is just a little bit different, a challenge to complete in just 30 minutes.

In our house, it's a rare meal that passes without some kind of cheese, whether it's at the beginning or end. Cheese is invaluable in creating light little first courses such as a plain lettuce salad upgraded with a crisp cheese biscuit, a *Parmesan Fricco*. This is one of several 'Parmesan Cheese Dreams' that I suggest. As for an easy ending to a meal, I often turn to fruit – grapes, apples, pears, peaches or whatever happens to be in season – and pair it with cheese if not part of another course. In an emergency, dried apricots and raisins are useful, plus whole almonds or hazelnuts, preferably with their skins. For more ambitious desserts, take a look in Fast Finishes (page 128). Many of them take only a few minutes.

Thirty Minutes to the Table

Roast Cod with Tropical Fruit Salsa

Fruit with fish was never my favourite partnership until I came across this recipe. It seems that the acid in wine and orange juice, backed by the zip of Dijon mustard, provides just the balance needed for the sweetness in fruit. Encouraged, I tried an alternative mix of cucumber with strawberries seasoned with balsamic vinegar, with equal success. Neither takes more than 10 minutes to make, so I invite you to take a gamble and see if our tastes agree. You'll find any firm fish is good cooked this way, including salmon and monkfish.

1 Light the barbecue. (In winter, simply roast the foil package of fish in a 180°C/350°F/Gas Mark 4 oven.) Whisk the wine, mustard and orange juice in a bowl with salt and pepper to taste. Lay the cod on a large piece of heavy-duty foil and fold up the sides. Brush the fish with oil, then pour over two-thirds of the marinade. Seal the foil. When the grill is hot, set the cod package to cook, allowing 10–12 minutes for pieces that are 2.5 cm/1 in thick.

2 Meanwhile, make the salsa: pare the peel from the mango and cut the flesh from the stone. Dice the flesh and put it in a bowl. Halve the papaya and scoop out the seeds with a spoon. Cut away the skin, dice the flesh and add it to the mango. Cut the peel, pith and skin away from the oranges and scoop out the segments. Dice them and add to the other fruit. Pour over the remaining marinade. Shred the basil leaves, reserving four sprigs for garnish. Stir the shredded basil into the salsa, taste and adjust the seasoning.

3 To finish: open the cod package and test the fish pieces with a fork – they should just flake easily. Transfer them to warm individual plates, spoon the salsa on the side, and top with a basil sprig.

Getting Ahead: Fruit salsa keeps well in the refrigerator for up to 4 hours, but roast the fish only just before serving.

On the Side: For the perfect summer supper, you could barbecue garden tomatoes and corn on the cob, side by side with the cod.

In the Glass: Some more of that full-bodied Chardonnay or Sémillon you've added to the marinade.

BARBECUED TOMATOES

Halve the tomatoes through the 'equator' and sprinkle cut sides with salt, pepper and a little sugar. Set the tomatoes, cut-sides down, on an oiled rack and grill until the juices run, 5–8 minutes. Turn them over and continue cooking until tender. Cooking time depends on their size and ripeness.

BARBECUED CORN ON THE COB

Strip back the husks on the corn cobs and discard the silk. Brush the corn with melted butter, sprinkle with salt and pepper. Fold back the husks to cover the ears. Grill, turning the corn often, until the kernels detach easily when tested with a knife, 10–15 minutes, depending on the heat of the grill.

Serves 4

250 ml/8 fl oz full-bodied white wine, such as Chardonnay or Sémillon
3 tablespoons honey mustard
175 ml/6 fl oz fresh orange juice
salt and pepper
4 portions cod fillet (about 675 g/1 1/2 lb)
1–2 tablespoons vegetable oil, for brushing

For the tropical fruit salsa
1 small ripe mango
1 small papaya (avocado-sized)
2 navel oranges
medium bunch of basil (about 40 g/1 1/2 oz)

STRAWBERRY AND CUCUMBER SALSA
(Makes 500 ml/16 fl oz, to serve 4)
This odd-sounding combination is utterly delicious with fish. Peel 1/2 a cucumber, halve it and scoop out the seeds. Cut the halves lengthwise in strips, then crosswise in small dice and mix with 1/2 teaspoon salt. Leave for 10–15 minutes to draw out juices. Hull 110 g/4 oz strawberries, washing only if they are sandy. Slice and put them in a bowl with 2 spring onions, sliced with the green tops. Rinse the cucumber, drain on paper towels and mix with the strawberries. Stir in 1 tablespoon balsamic vinegar and 2 tablespoons chopped mint or parsley. Season to taste with sugar, salt and pepper. Serve at room temperature.

Vodka and Sesame Salmon with Parsley Salad

I've a weakness for the smoky flavours of toasted sesame, a perfect match for salmon sharpened with a sprinkling of lime, then flamed with vodka. With the salmon comes a salad of fresh parsley, dressed with oil and lime juice; it's delicious too with other fish and chicken.

1 Cut the salmon into four equal pieces so they take the same time to cook. Lay them in a non-metallic dish and sprinkle with 2 tablespoons of the vodka and some salt and pepper. Turn and sprinkle the other sides with a tablespoon of vodka and more salt and pepper. Leave them to marinate for 10–15 minutes so they pickle slightly and pick up taste.

2 Meanwhile, toast the sesame seeds in a dry non-stick frying pan over medium heat, stirring often, until they are brown and fragrant, 4–5 minutes.

3 Make the parsley salad: reserve 2 tablespoons of lime juice. Whisk the remaining juice in a small bowl with the oil, and a little salt and pepper. Pull the parsley sprigs from the stems and discard the stems. Rinse the sprigs in cold water and dry on paper towels or using a salad spinner. Add the parsley to the lime dressing and toss to mix. Taste and adjust the seasoning.

4 Drain the salmon and pat it dry on paper towels. Melt the butter in a frying pan. Sauté the salmon until browned, 2–3 minutes. For an attractive golden brown it's best to heat the butter until spluttering stops, then put in the salmon with the cut- or backbone-side downwards. When brown, sprinkle it with the chopped garlic, then turn and continue cooking. Depending on the fillets' thickness, this should take 2–3 minutes for medium done salmon that is still translucent in the centre, or 4–5 minutes if you prefer it well done.

5 Pour the remaining vodka into the pan, bring just to the boil, then set it alight, standing well back. Take the pan from the heat and sprinkle the salmon with the reserved lime juice, sesame oil and sesame seeds. Arrange the salmon on warm plates and spoon over the pan juices. Garnish the plates with parsley salad and lime wedges.

On the Side: A *Parmesan Fricco* or one of my *Aunt Louie's Cheese Balls* (page 27).

In the Glass: A lemon-tinged Sauvignon Blanc, or just possibly a tot of ice-cold vodka.

Serves 4

675 g/1¹/₂ lb salmon fillet, skinned
5–6 tablespoons vodka
salt and pepper
2 tablespoons sesame seeds
60 g/2 oz butter
2 garlic cloves, finely chopped
1 teaspoon dark sesame oil
1 lime, cut in wedges, for serving

For the parsley salad
juice of 1 lime
3 tablespoons vegetable oil
large bunch of flatleaf parsley
  (about 90 g/3 oz)

Tea-smoked Salmon with Rémoulade Sauce

Simple home smokers that go on the top of the stove are easy to find, or improvise by setting a round steamer rack in a wok, covering it with a lid for smoking. For the smoke flavour, take your pick of fragrant teas such as jasmine, orange pekoe or apple, or use your favourite wood chips.

Serves 4

675 g/1¹/₂ lb skinless salmon fillet
60 g/2 oz brown sugar
2 tablespoons sea salt
2 tablespoons leaf tea

For the rémoulade sauce
250 ml/8 fl oz mayonnaise
3 gherkins, chopped
2 tablespoons capers, chopped
1 anchovy fillet, finely chopped
1 teaspoon Dijon mustard
1 tablespoon chopped parsley
1 tablespoon chopped tarragon
salt and pepper

home smoker or wok with lid and
  steamer rack

1 To remove pin bones, run your thumb along the centre of the salmon fillet towards the tail to feel for bones. If they are not already removed, pull them out with tweezers. Cut the fish in four even pieces and measure their thickness with a ruler: holding the ruler upright, measure the fish at its thickest point. For cooking time, allow 8–10 minutes per 2.5 cm/1 in. Most salmon fillets are about 2 cm/³/₄ in thick and thus take 6–8 minutes for medium done salmon, 2 minutes longer for well done. Mix the sugar and salt and use to coat the salmon. Cover and chill it for at least 10 minutes. Pour cold water to cover the tea leaves and let them soak.

2 For the rémoulade sauce: stir all the ingredients together in a bowl, taste and adjust the seasoning. Cover and chill.

3 Drain the tea and sprinkle it over the bottom of the smoker. Oil the smoker rack and set it in the smoker. Rinse the salmon fillets, dry on paper towels, and set them on the rack so they do not touch each other. Set the smoker on a burner over medium heat. When you see the first wisps of smoke, close the top of the smoker or cover it tightly with foil. Cook for 6–10 minutes, depending on how you like your salmon done.

4 Take the smoker from the heat and leave for 3–5 minutes before opening so the smoke subsides. Test the salmon with a fork – it should be transparent in the centre, or just flake easily, as you prefer. Serve it at room temperature or warm, with rémoulade sauce in a separate bowl.

Getting Ahead: For more intense taste, the salmon can be marinated in sugar and salt for up to an hour, and the rémoulade sauce mellows agreeably if you make it an hour or two in advance.

In the Glass: A chilled Chardonnay is a perfect partner for the taste of smoke.

TO SMOKE ON A BARBECUE
Smoking is equally easy on the barbecue. Soak a handful of wood chips (sawdust is too fine) for a half hour. Meanwhile light the barbecue. Prepare the fish as above and set it on the grill rack. Drain the wood chips and sprinkle them over the hot coals. Add the grill rack with the fish and cover the barbecue with the lid or foil. Smoke for 6–l0 minutes – the fillets should just flake easily when tested with a fork.

Mussel Stew with Saffron and Cream

We once had a summer house near Dieppe, on the Normandy coast, and ever since I have loved mussels. Saffron is a natural partner for fish – it colours this fragrant stew a glowing orange-gold. Try substituting clams for the mussels, but allow more time for them to open over the heat as their shells are thicker.

1 Put the wine and shallots in a large soup pot and stir in the saffron threads. Cover and simmer for 2 minutes. Rinse the mussels under cold running water and pull off the 'beards' with a small knife. Discard any open shells that do not close when tapped on the counter. Stir the mussels into the pot, cover and continue cooking just until the shells open, 4–5 minutes, stirring once or twice. Note: if overcooked, the mussels will be tough.

2 Remove the mussels with a slotted spoon and discard any that have not opened. Pour the cooking liquid into a bowl, leaving grit behind. Wipe out the pot, pour the cooking liquid back, and stir in the cream and chervil or parsley. Simmer for 1–2 minutes, taste and adjust the seasoning – salt may not be needed. Stir the mussels into the liquid, heat gently for 1 minute, and spoon the mussels and liquid into large bowls. Serve them at once, very hot, with bowls on the side for discarded shells.

Serves 4

500 ml/16 fl oz dry white wine
6 shallots, chopped
big pinch of saffron threads
1.35 kg/3 lb mussels, washed
500 ml/16 fl oz single cream
bunch of chervil or flatleaf parsley
  (about 60 g/2 oz), chopped
salt and pepper

Getting Ahead: Wash the mussels up to an hour ahead, but cook them just before serving.

On the Side: Baguette or *Cracked Wheat Bread* (page 49) for soaking up the fragrant cooking juices.

In the Glass: A dry white Sauvignon Blanc or a Muscadet.

Trout Fillets with a Crispy Topping

Fishing is a national sport in France and in summer the river banks are lined with anglers hoping to catch their supper. This recipe comes from Eric, our computer guru, who spends any idle moment with rod, line, and wriggling worm. Trout may be a rarity, but perch and even pike are a reward for his patience.

Serves 4

75 g/2¹/₂ oz butter

4 plump trout or other fish fillets (such as lemon sole) with or without skin

salt and pepper

2–3 garlic cloves, chopped

1 onion, chopped

2 teaspoons ground cumin

1 teaspoon ground coriander

1 teaspoon dried thyme

2 tablespoons mild or hot smooth Dijon mustard

100 g/3¹/₂ oz browned breadcrumbs

3–4 tablespoons chopped parsley

juice of 1 lemon

1 Heat the oven to 180°C/350°F/Gas Mark 4. Melt the butter in a small pan – we'll use it three ways. First brush a baking dish large enough to take the fillets without overlapping. Lay the fillets in the dish, brush with more butter and sprinkle with salt and pepper.

2 For the topping, fry the garlic and onion in the remaining melted butter until soft and fragrant, 2–3 minutes. Stir in the cumin, coriander and thyme, and cook for 1 minute – this develops their flavours and they'll be wonderfully fragrant. Take from the heat, stir in the mustard, breadcrumbs and parsley and spoon the mixture over the fish.

3 Bake until the topping is browned and the fish just flakes easily when tested with a fork, 15–25 minutes depending on thickness. Serve the trout very hot in the baking dish, or at room temperature, sprinkling with lemon juice just before serving.

Getting Ahead: The trout and topping can be prepared up to 2 hours ahead, then baked at the last minute.

On the Side: I enjoy this trout served hot with buttered cabbage, or served at room temperature, Mediterranean-style, with a side dish of ratatouille.

In the Glass: Any simple dry white wine.

Moroccan Couscous Salad with Spicy Sausage

Traditionally couscous salad (or tabbouleh) is one of many little dishes of mezze, the appetizers that open all Middle Eastern meals, but I also enjoy it with kebabs or the spicy Moroccan lamb sausages called merguez. *Any spicy sausage can be substituted here.*

1 Put the couscous in a large bowl and pour over the amount of boiling water indicated on the package. Cover and leave it to soak and soften, about 15 minutes. Heat a tablespoon of the oil in a frying pan and add the sausages. Prick them with a fork so they do not burst. Fry them over medium heat, turning often, until brown and the juice runs clear, not pink, when the sausages are pierced with the fork, 7–10 minutes depending on their size. If cooked too fast they will burst, though personally I don't mind.

2 Meanwhile, prepare the tomatoes (the riper the better), spring onions, parsley and mint and mix them together in a bowl. Stir in the coriander, cumin and lemon zest, with salt and pepper. Stir this mixture into the couscous, using a fork. Stir in the lemon juice and the remaining olive oil, taste the couscous and adjust seasoning. Serve it at room temperature. with the hot spicy sausages on the side.

Getting Ahead: You'll be glad to know that this couscous salad improves on keeping for up to two days in the refrigerator, so make it in advance, and keep any leftovers.

On the Side: Morocco grows lots of oranges, and a salad of sliced oranges would be just the right balance for tabbouleh and *merguez*.

In the Glass: A no-name hearty red like those of Morocco.

SAUSAGES WITH GRAPES
(Serves 4)
This makes a handy little appetizer or light main dish. Allow about 170 g/6 oz mild or spicy sausages per person and fry them as in *Couscous Salad*. Remove and set them aside. Add a cup of red or green grapes per person to the pan and cook over medium heat, shaking the pan often, for 2–3 minutes until one or two grapes burst. Replace the sausages, sprinkle with a teaspoon or more of balsamic vinegar per serving, and cook for a further 1–2 minutes so the flavours blend.

Serves 4

170 g/6 oz instant couscous
boiling water for soaking
125 ml/4 fl oz olive oil
675 g/1$^{1}/_{2}$ lb *merguez* or other spicy
  sausages
330 g/12 oz tomatoes, seeded and
  chopped (including peel)
3 spring onions, thinly sliced with
  green tops
60 g/2 oz parsley sprigs, chopped
60 g/2 oz mint leaves, chopped
1 teaspoon ground coriander
$^{1}/_{2}$ teaspoon ground cumin
grated zest of 1 lemon
salt and pepper
125 ml/4 fl oz lemon juice

Flat Omelette with Onion, Pepper and Chilli

A Mexican-style omelette, browned on both sides and served as a flat cake, can be served hot or at room temperature with all sorts of fillings. This combination of onion with sweet and hot peppers is classic.

1 Heat half the oil in the omelette pan and fry the onion until soft, 3–5 minutes. Add the pepper and cook also until soft, 3–4 minutes longer. Stir in the garlic, chilli and tomato with salt and pepper and continue cooking for 3–4 minutes, stirring often, until excess liquid has evaporated. Stir in the coriander or parsley, taste and adjust the seasoning – the mixture should be intensely flavoured to balance the delicate eggs. Transfer it to a bowl and wipe out the pan with paper towels.

2 Whisk the eggs in a bowl with a little salt and pepper until frothy; stir in the pepper mixture. Heat the remaining oil in the pan over medium heat and add the egg mixture. Stir the eggs briskly with a fork until they start to thicken. With the fork, lift the edges of the omelette so that the uncooked egg runs underneath. Continue cooking without stirring until the omelette is firm on top and browned underneath, about 2 minutes.

3 Turn the omelette on to a heatproof plate. Slide it back into the pan and brown the other side. Cut it in wedges to serve hot or at room temperature.

Getting Ahead: Cook the omelette filling up to 2 hours ahead; it will be fine kept covered at room temperature. Fry the omelette just before serving.

On the Side: In echo of Mexican refried beans, heat a can of cooked black or red kidney beans in a couple of tablespoons lard or oil. Crush them with a fork and stir in 2–3 tablespoons grated Cheddar.

In the Glass: What else but a generous measure of chilled Mexican beer.

Serves 2

2 tablespoons olive oil

1 medium onion, thinly sliced

1 medium red or green pepper, cored, seeded and sliced

2 garlic cloves, chopped

1/2 jalapeño or red chilli, seeded and finely chopped

1 medium tomato, peeled, seeded and chopped (page 166)

salt and pepper

2 tablespoons chopped coriander or parsley

4–5 eggs

23 cm/9 in non-stick omelette pan

Steak Marchand de Vin

One of my first memories of a good French meal involves Steak Marchand de Vin. *Too late for lunch, I stopped one day at a bar where steak-frites was the only choice. The proprietor took out his pan and fried up fresh steaks as I watched, fascinated. After a quick sizzle on each side, he transferred the meat to plates and went to work on the sauce. In went a dusting of chopped shallots and garlic, and then came the wine, poured from an open, unlabelled bottle. But we were in Burgundy, and that bottle had a pedigree. Before my eyes the wine was boiled almost to a glaze to concentrate and mellow the flavour – the key step, I discovered, when I tried it myself. Fresh herbs and cubes of cold butter, swirled in the warm sauce until melted, completed the dish.*

Serves 4

4 individual steaks, cut 2 cm/¾ in thick, such as
  fillet, T-bone, French entrecôte (rib)
salt and pepper
3 tablespoons vegetable oil
2 shallots, chopped
2 garlic cloves, chopped
300 ml/10 fl oz red wine
2 tablespoons chopped curly parsley
1 tablespoon snipped chives
1 tablespoon chopped tarragon or basil
2 tablespoons cold butter, cut in pieces

1 Season the steaks on both sides with pepper and a very small pinch of salt. Heat half the oil in a heavy frying pan, add the steaks and fry over a high heat for about 2 minutes, until brown. Turn the steaks, lower the heat to medium, and continue cooking for 2–5 minutes, depending on their thickness and how well you like them done. To test the cooking of a steak, press the meat in the centre with your finger (don't worry, it won't burn you). If soft, the steak is rare, if slightly resistant, the meat will be medium, and if firm it is well done (and likely to be dry). Remove the steaks to a dish, cover with foil and keep warm.

2 Heat the remaining oil in the pan, add the shallots and the garlic and fry, stirring for 1–2 minutes until they begin to brown. Pour in the wine and simmer for 2–3 minutes, stirring and scraping to dissolve the pan juices, until the wine is reduced almost to a glaze. Stir in the parsley, chives, tarragon or basil and any juices that have run from the meat. Take the pan off the heat. Whisk in the butter a few pieces at a time so that it softens and thickens the sauce without melting to oil. Taste and adjust the seasoning, spoon the sauce over the steaks and serve at once.

On the Side: We must have some chips, cut skinny the way the French like them, and add a green salad if you like.

In the Glass: Pour your favourite red wine, bearing in mind that one glass for a prime steak will probably not be enough. If you are planning on something simple, by all means use the same wine when you make the sauce but, if this is a special bottle, keep it strictly for drinking. The nuances of a fine vintage will be lost as soon as the wine is heated.

Steak Marchand de Vin is a basic recipe that is wonderfully easy to vary.

MEDITERRANEAN STEAK MARCHAND DE VIN
Omit the chives and tarragon and use flatleaf instead of curly parsley. Double the amount of garlic and add a finely chopped anchovy fillet with the red wine.

STEAK DIJONNAISE
Substitute white wine, preferably Chardonnay, for the red wine. After adding the herbs, take from the heat and whisk in 1 tablespoon Dijon mustard and 150 ml/5 fl oz double cream. Bring the sauce just back to the boil, take off the heat and whisk in the butter. Taste and adjust the seasoning, adding more mustard if you like.

Medallions of Pork Dijonnaise

Bacon and mustard, salty and hot, have long been happy partners and this cream sauce binds them together. To speed cooking, I'm suggesting you buy a piece of boneless pork loin, and cut it into steaks; pork chops are an alternative but will take a few minutes longer because of the bone.

1 Cut the pork loin in eight even slices – the thickness will vary with the diameter of the piece of meat. Put the flour on a plate and season with salt and pepper. Dip the medallions in the flour, lift out and pat them so they are evenly coated.

2 Heat the oil in a frying pan and fry the bacon until browned, 2–3 minutes. Remove it, add the medallions to the pan and brown them well, allowing 2–3 minutes on each side. Remove them and set aside.

3 Pour the wine into the pan and simmer until reduced by half, 2–3 minutes. Stir in the stock and bacon and add the bouquet garni. Simmer until the sauce is lightly thickened and reduced by half, about 5 minutes. Whisk in the cream and simmer for 1 minute. Whisk the mustard into the sauce, off the heat, taste and adjust the seasoning. (If mustard cooks at high heat, it turns bitter.) Replace the medallions and very gently heat for 4–5 minutes. The meat should feel firm when you press it with a fingertip, showing it is well done.

4 Discard the bouquet garni. Lift out the medallions, and arrange them on a warm serving dish or on plates. Spoon over the sauce and sprinkle with parsley.

Getting Ahead: *Medallions Dijonnaise* can be cooked and kept up to a day in the refrigerator. Reheat the pork very gently on top of the stove until hot, taking care not to overcook and toughen it. Sprinkle with parsley just before serving.

On the Side: In Dijon if I'm lucky, this dish comes with a crisp potato cake, but boiled rice or pasta is a perfectly acceptable alternative. A few sprigs of watercress on each plate will add colour.

In the Glass: Let's keep the style Burgundian with a cool-climate Chardonnay from New Zealand or Chile.

Serves 4

900 g/2 lb boneless pork loin
2–3 tablespoons plain white flour
salt and pepper
2 tablespoons vegetable oil
125 g/4$^{1}/_{2}$ oz thickly sliced bacon, diced
175 ml/6 fl oz dry white wine
250 ml/8 fl oz chicken stock, more if needed
bouquet garni of parsley stalks, 2–3 sprigs
  thyme and 1 bay leaf, tied with string
125 ml/4 fl oz crème fraîche or double cream
1 tablespoon Dijon mustard, or to taste
1 tablespoon chopped parsley

Hot Toddy Chicken Breasts

When you add whisky to a pan of chicken breasts, it makes a fine blaze. The whisky flavour lingers in the pan juices, making a tasty sauce with lemon and honey – the classic trio in a hot toddy.

Serves 4

4 boneless, skinless chicken breasts

3 tablespoons plain white flour

grated zest and juice of 1 large lemon

salt and pepper

30 g/1 oz butter

2 tablespoons olive oil

90 ml/3 fl oz whisky

2 teaspoons clear honey

125 ml/4 fl oz chicken stock

For the sautéed radicchio

2 radicchio heads

1 tablespoon vegetable oil

100 g/3½ oz streaky bacon, cut into
  strips

1 Lay the chicken breasts on a chopping board and cut each diagonally into three slices. Put the slices between two sheets of clingfilm and pound with a rolling pin to about 3 mm/1/8 in thickness. Mix the flour on a plate with the lemon zest, salt and pepper. Coat the chicken in flour and pat to discard the excess.

2 Heat half the butter and oil a medium frying pan. Sauté half the chicken for 1–2 minutes until browned, then turn and brown the other side. Transfer the chicken to a plate. Melt the remaining butter and oil and fry the rest.

3 Return all the chicken to the pan, add the whisky and heat for 1/2–1 minute. Set it alight, standing back from the flames, then keep cooking until they die down. Transfer the chicken to a serving dish and keep it warm.

4 Cook the radicchio: shred the radicchio, discarding the white core. Heat the oil in a frying pan. Fry the bacon until it starts to brown. Add the radicchio and some black pepper and cook, stirring for 1–2 minutes until it wilts, but is still a bit crisp. Taste and season; cover with foil and keep warm.

5 Stir the lemon juice and honey into the pan with the stock. Simmer until slightly thickened, stirring to dissolve the juices, 1–2 minutes. Taste and adjust the seasoning. Serve the chicken with the sauce and radicchio.

Getting Ahead: Slice and pound the chicken up to 4 hours ahead, storing it in the refrigerator. Coat it with flour and fry it just before serving.

On the Side: The bitter tinge of the sautéed radicchio makes a pleasant contrast to the honey sauce. Try other bitter leaves too, such as chicory or escarole.

In the Glass: Please try a dark beer, served at room temperature if you seek authentic Scottish taste!

Taiwanese Chicken Stir Fry

This chicken is typical of the lively little dishes served in the outdoor markets of Asia. Whether or not to spice it with chilli is your choice.

Serves 2

2 boneless, skinless chicken breasts

small bunch of Thai basil or coriander

2 tablespoons vegetable oil

3 spring onions, sliced with the green tops

3 garlic cloves, chopped

2.5 cm/1 in piece of fresh root ginger,
chopped

1 small green or red chilli, cored, seeded and
finely chopped (optional)

1 tablespoon soy sauce, more to taste

3 tablespoons rice wine

1 teaspoon sugar

1 tablespoon dark sesame oil

1 Cut the chicken breasts into 6 mm/$^1/_4$ in slices across the grain of the meat. Pull basil or coriander leaves from the stems and shred the leaves.

2 Heat the vegetable oil in a wok or deep frying pan over high heat. Add the spring onions, garlic, ginger and chilli if you are using it, and stir fry them, tossing and turning vigorously. Cook them just until fragrant, about 1 minute, and do not let them brown. Stir in the chicken and stir fry just until white, $^1/_2$–1 minute. Stir in the soy sauce, followed by the rice wine and sugar. Note that brisk frying so the ingredients cook evenly is important.

3 Lower the heat to medium – now you can relax a bit. Simmer the chicken, stirring often, until it is very tender and has absorbed most of the liquid, 5–7 minutes. Stir in the sesame oil and basil or coriander, taste for seasoning, and serve the chicken at once.

Getting Ahead: Prepare the ingredients up to 2 hours ahead, keeping them in the refrigerator.

On the Side: On a warm evening, *Taiwanese Chicken Stir Fry* is excellent as a warm salad, served on crisp lettuce. On cooler days, a bowl of Asian-style boiled rice or crispy noodles would be in order.

In the Glass: Go for a chilled beer.

Chicken Breasts with Juniper and White Wine

The cooks of the Burgundian town of Chablis, famous for its white wine, like to cook meats in a rich white wine sauce with juniper berries and shallots. I tried it one day with chicken breasts, great winter fare!

1 Split the chicken breasts horizontally into two even slices. Season them on both sides with salt and pepper and set them in a frying pan. Cover them with stock, adding more if needed. Cover and simmer the chicken very gently until tender when pierced with a two-pronged fork, 8–10 minutes.

2 Meanwhile start the sauce: put the juniper berries and peppercorns in a plastic bag and crush with a heavy pan or rolling pin (or do this with a pestle in a mortar). Put the crushed spices in a small pan, add the vinegar and boil for 2–3 minutes until reduced by half. Pour in the wine and boil for 3–5 minutes until reduced by half again.

3 When the chicken is done, transfer it to a plate, reserving the cooking liquid. To complete the sauce, melt the butter in a saucepan, add the shallots or onion and sauté them for 1–2 minutes until soft but not brown. Stir in the flour and cook until it binds. Pour in the cooking liquid and bring the sauce to the boil, whisking all the time until it thickens. Add the reduced wine mixture and whisk in the tomato purée, cream, salt and pepper. Simmer the sauce until it coats the back of a spoon, 2–3 minutes. Taste and adjust the seasoning.

4 Return the chicken to the sauce, pushing the pieces down so that they are completely covered. Cover and heat gently for 2–3 minutes so the flavours blend before serving.

Short Cut: This sauce also works well with leftover pieces of roast chicken. Simply bake the chicken in the sauce until piping hot for a quick supper dish.

On the Side: New potatoes boiled in their skins.

In the Glass: A white wine in the style of Chablis, that is to say a flinty Chardonnay. I'm happy to say there are more and more of them around.

Serves 4

4 boneless, skinless chicken breasts
salt and pepper
300 ml/10 fl oz chicken stock, more if needed

For the sauce
1 teaspoon juniper berries
1 teaspoon black peppercorns
3 tablespoons white wine vinegar
250 ml/8 fl oz dry white wine, such as
  Chardonnay
30 g/1 oz butter
3 shallots or 1 medium onion, finely chopped
2 tablespoons plain white flour
2 teaspoons tomato purée
3–4 tablespoons double cream

●Parmesan Cheese Dreams

Like most of us, I was brought up on Cheddar cheese – good stuff in its way but summed up by the expression 'mousetrap'. So for me a whole new world opened up when I first tasted Parmesan. I invested in a small tub of the freshly grated cheese and sprinkled it on my supper of green salad, where it mingled intriguingly with the vinaigrette dressing. Next I bought a whole chunk and scattered luscious, slightly crunchy curls of Parmesan on everything from prosciutto to beef carpaccio to marinated tuna and all sorts of vegetables. I soon found that Parmesan could help in many a kitchen crisis. Here are a few ideas.

Stracchiatella (Serves 2)

The name means 'rag' and describes the shreds that form when egg and grated Parmesan are whisked into boiling broth. If you are using canned chicken broth for this, make sure it is low in salt.

Bring 500 ml/16 fl oz chicken broth to the boil. In a small bowl, whisk together 1 egg, 1–2 tablespoons of grated Parmesan and a generous grating of nutmeg. When the broth is boiling, add the egg mixture in a steady stream, whisking constantly. The egg will cook into strings or 'rags'. Stir for about 30 seconds longer so that the egg does not clump and then taste, adjust the seasoning and serve.

Aunt Louie's Cheese Balls (Makes about 30)

My Yorkshire aunt was famous for these cheese balls, which, when bitten into, would explode in the faces of the unwary at cocktail parties. Try them with a dry martini.

In a bowl mix 125 g/4½ oz plain white flour, 110 g/4 oz grated Parmesan and a ½ teaspoon each of salt, pepper and dry mustard. Stir in 110 g/4 oz of melted butter so the mixture forms breadcrumbs and press it into balls the size of walnuts (if very dry, add a little more butter). Set the balls on a buttered baking sheet and chill for 30 minutes. Heat the oven to 180°C/350°F/ Gas Mark 4 and bake the cheese balls until lightly browned, 15–20 minutes. They keep well in an airtight container.

Parmesan Fricco (Makes 8 wafers)

I love these crisp wafers as a quick cocktail nibble or lively accompaniment to a summer salad, or try them sandwiched with chicken salad, sliced avocado and tomato for a spectacular main dish. Just one ingredient, Parmesan cheese, is needed!

Heat the oven to 190°C/375°F/Gas Mark 5 and line a baking sheet with buttered greaseproof paper. Finely grate about 110 g/4 oz Parmesan cheese. Drop about 2 tablespoons at a time on to the baking sheet and repeat to make 4–5 mounds, spacing them well apart. Flatten to 7.5 cm/3 in rounds with the back of the spoon. Bake until golden, 4–6 minutes; they should be brown but not dark, or they will taste bitter. Slide the paper on to a work surface and let the wafers cool slightly. Transfer them to a rack to cool completely and crispen. Let the baking sheet cool and then repeat to use the remaining cheese. Store the wafers in an airtight container.

Chicken Breasts en Cocotte with Lemon and Parmesan (Serves 2)

In this recipe, Parmesan performs the double function of flavouring and thickening a sauce for chicken breasts.

Heat the oven to 180°C/350°F/Gas Mark 4. Split 2 chicken breasts horizontally into two even slices and sprinkle with salt and pepper. Brown them in a tablespoon each of oil and butter in an ovenproof skillet or shallow casserole, allowing 2–3 minutes on each side. Add the pared zest of 1 lemon, cover and bake until tender and no pink juice runs when the breasts are pierced with the point of a knife, 6–8 minutes. Transfer the chicken to a warm serving dish, cover and keep warm. Boil the cooking juices until reduced to a dark glaze and then discard excess fat. Stir in 125 ml/4 fl oz double cream and bring to the boil, stirring to dissolve the pan juices. Strain this sauce into a small pan and whisk in 2 tablespoons grated Parmesan cheese. Bring the sauce just to a boil, whisking until it thickens a little. Take from the heat, taste and adjust the seasoning and pour it over the chicken.

TIPS FOR PARMESAN

Good Parmesan is aged for a year and a half or more. The cut surface must be moist but not beaded with sweat and a pale amber colour. A thick white layer under the rind is a sign of poorly stored dry cheese. Parmesan is best stored in large pieces in the refrigerator, tightly covered but not vacuum packed.

Grated Parmesan loses its fragrance rapidly and is best freshly grated. Try to find a microplane grater – it looks like a desk ruler and reduces hard cheese to a cloud of shavings with very little effort.

For intriguing flavour, try tucking a mixture of grated Parmesan and chopped flatleaf parsley bound with melted butter under the skin of a roast chicken – you'll need surprisingly little.

Include a chopped garlic clove in the same mixture of grated Parmesan and parsley bound with melted butter and top a thick fillet of cod or salmon, or a rack of lamb, before roasting in the oven.

Add a few tablespoons of grated Parmesan to a breadcrumb coating for vegetable fritters, potato croquettes and, above all, escalopes of veal.

Dishes cooked in a single pot are by definition simple affairs, often a matter of layering ingredients and simmering them all together to a triumphant, savoury finish. Alternatively, the components are added little by little, so that at the end of cooking everything is just tender and at its best. Often meat and other key ingredients are browned to develop a touch of caramel, then removed and put back later in the process.

One-pot recipes may be simple, yet they include some of the world's great dishes such as French daube of lamb. When I look at the list, I'm struck by their regional roots, conveying a strong sense of place. *Moroccan Tajine of Chicken with Aubergine* could only come from North Africa, and ratatouille is an instant glimpse of the Mediterranean sun. You will find inspiration for your next dinner party here, as well as family fare for every day. What is more, many single-pot recipes can be cooked ahead, then reheated. In fact often they benefit from a day or two's rest in the refrigerator, where the flavours blend and mellow.

Many of my one-pot ideas make a full meal, and where they don't I've suggested an accompaniment such as polenta or rice. Much depends on what you personally prefer, whether a starch or perhaps a salad. We in the west tend to turn to bread to round out a meal – in this chapter you'll see 'The Best of Breads', both of them a bit out of the ordinary. One is crunchy with cracked wheat, the other is dark with molasses.

Lastly, a note on equipment. I find that the most versatile single pot is a sturdy, heavy casserole – ideally the food should fill it by about two-thirds. Too small a pan is an endless frustration as stirring and whisking are awkward, while in too large a pan the ingredients tend to dry and scorch. So if you do much cooking you'll need casseroles in at least two sizes. The other invaluable pan is a traditional cast-iron skillet, preferably with a non-stick or enamel finish and an ovenproof handle. A French-style sauté pan or simply a very deep frying pan serve the same purpose. All these skillet-type pans can be used for frying, for shallow-cooked dishes, typically of chicken pieces or chops, and for gratins that are browned on top.

One-pot Ideas

Summer Herb Soup with Nettles and Sunflower Seeds

This recipe comes from an idealistic young French chef, François Bogard, at the Château de Chaumont in the Loire valley. His ingredients are left to grow naturally with only organic fertilizer and the minimum of irrigation, and in his recipes even the water comes from a bottle so he knows the source. There's nothing Spartan, however, about his use of cream! Sorrel or watercress can be substituted for nettles, and the soup can be served hot or cold.

1 Pull leaves from the greens and herbs, discarding the stems (wear rubber gloves when handling the nettles). Wash them and drain in a colander. Bring salted water to the boil in the pot, add the spinach, rocket, nettles and parsley and bring just back to the boil. Drain, rinse the greens with cold water and leave to drain thoroughly. Chop the mint leaves, reserving six sprigs for decoration.

2 Wipe out the pot and melt the butter in it, then add the spring onions and sauté until soft. Pour in the water and bring to the boil. Add the peas and boil them until tender, 5–7 minutes or longer if your peas are a bit elderly. Transfer them to a bowl of cold water with a draining spoon.

3 Add the cream to the cooking liquid and bring it just to the boil. Stir in the drained greens.

4 Purée the soup in the food processor or blender. Bring it just back to the boil and add the drained peas, chopped mint, celery salt and pepper. Taste and adjust the seasoning. Serve the soup hot or chilled (if chilled, it will need more seasoning), sprinkled with toasted sunflower seeds and topped with a mint sprig.

Getting Ahead: After the soup has been puréed, it can be kept for a day in the refrigerator, or frozen for a month. To finish it, bring it to the boil, add the peas and other ingredients and continue as directed.

On the Side: Try *Aunt Louie's Cheese Balls* (page 27).

In the Glass: A white wine such as a Riesling or dry Chenin Blanc.

Serves 6

140 g/5 oz baby spinach

140 g/5 oz rocket

110 g/4 oz young stinging nettles

medium bunch of flatleaf parsley (about 60 g/2 oz)

medium bunch of peppermint or spearmint (about 60 g/2 oz)

22 g/³/4 oz butter

2 spring onions, chopped with some of the green tops

1 litre/1³/4 pints still mineral water

110 g/4 oz shelled fresh or frozen peas

1 litre/1³/4 pints double cream

1/2 teaspoon celery salt

salt and pepper

75 g/2¹/2 oz toasted sunflower seeds

large, heavy-based soup pot
food processor or blender

Winter Celery and Stilton Soup with Herb Dumplings

Born and bred in England, how could I not love soup with Stilton cheese? As a child, my mother had spent her holidays on a farm that made champion Stilton cheese and at home we benefited from her happy memories.

Serves 6

45 g/1½ oz butter

2 onions, thinly sliced

small bunch of celery (about 280 g/10 oz), thinly sliced

salt and pepper

2 potatoes, peeled and thinly sliced

1 litre/1¾ pints chicken stock

250 ml/8 fl oz single cream

170 g/6 oz Stilton cheese, crumbled

125 ml/4 fl oz white port, more if you wish

few celery leaves (for decoration)

For the dumplings

450 g/1 lb loaf sliced white bread, more if needed

250 ml/8 fl oz milk, more if needed

2 tablespoons chopped sage or parsley

2 eggs, whisked until frothy

large, heavy-based soup pot

food processor or blender

1 Melt the butter in the pot and stir in the onions, celery, salt and pepper. Press a piece of foil on the vegetables, cover the pot, and cook over very low heat, stirring occasionally, until the vegetables are tender, 25–30 minutes. Do not let them colour as we want the soup to be white.

2 Remove about half the vegetables and set them aside. Stir in the potatoes and stock, cover and simmer the soup for 25–30 minutes.

3 Meanwhile, make the dumplings: cut the bread in cubes, discarding the crusts. Put the bread in a bowl, pour over the milk and leave to soak for 5–10 minutes. Stir to break up the bread. Chop the reserved vegetables and stir them into the bread with the sage or parsley, salt and pepper. Taste and adjust the seasoning. Stir in the eggs and leave the mixture to stand and thicken somewhat, 10–15 minutes.

4 Purée the soup in the processor or blender. Strain it into a bowl to remove fibres. Wipe out the pot, pour back the soup and stir in the cream, cheese and port. Heat gently, stirring, until the cheese melts and the soup is smooth. Taste and adjust the seasoning.

5 To cook the dumplings: the mixture should just hold a shape – if too thin, stir in more bread, or if thick, add a little milk. Drop generous spoonfuls of the mixture on top of the soup and poach over low heat until they are firm, 8–10 minutes. Do not let the soup boil or the cheese may cook into strings. Ladle the soup and dumplings into warm bowls and top with a celery leaf. If you like, add an extra spoonful of port to each bowl of soup at the table.

Shortcut: Omit the dumplings – the soup is lighter and still delicious.

Getting Ahead: Make the soup but do not add the cheese. Store it for up to 24 hours, covered, in the refrigerator. When serving, bring the soup just back to the boil, add the cheese and heat gently just until it melts; do not let it boil. Make dumplings and cook as directed just before serving.

On the Side: A crisp *Parmesan Fricco* (page 27).

In the Glass: A measure of warming port, a natural with blue Stilton cheese.

Russian Cabbage Soup

My husband's family came from Russia, so it's no surprise that our son, Simon, took to Russia like a native when he moved there a dozen years ago. In Russia you can always rely on splendid bowls of soup and here are two of them, a lesser known cabbage soup called shchi, *and the famous beetroot soup,* bortsch. *In Russia, simmering soup is a leisurely business taking at least a day, so here I'm suggesting you use canned beef or chicken broth to save time.* Shchi *can be made with fresh or pickled cabbage (sauerkraut) and I like to use both.*

Serves 8

1 small head white cabbage (about 900 g/2 lb)

2 tablespoons beef dripping or vegetable oil

2 onions, sliced

2 carrots, sliced

3 garlic cloves, chopped

2.5 litres/4^1/2 pints canned beef or chicken broth

2.5 litres/4^1/2 pints water

1 large potato, peeled and diced

330 g/12 oz fresh or canned sauerkraut, rinsed
  and drained

30 g/1 oz chopped pickled mushrooms or
  110 g/4 oz button mushrooms, chopped and
  stirred with 2 tablespoons wine vinegar

salt and pepper

1–2 tablespoons wine vinegar (optional)

For serving

2–3 tablespoons chopped dill

250 ml/8 fl oz sour cream

large, heavy-based soup pot

1 Coarsely shred the cabbage, discarding the core. Heat the dripping or oil in the soup pot, add the onions and carrots and sauté over medium heat until soft, 5–8 minutes. Stir in the garlic and cook until fragrant. Stir in the broth and water, potato, cabbage, sauerkraut and pickled mushrooms or fresh mushrooms and vinegar, with salt and pepper. Cover, bring to the boil and simmer the soup until the cabbage is tender, 50–60 minutes. Taste and adjust the seasoning, adding vinegar if you prefer a tart flavour. The soup should be packed with vegetables and taste rich so, if necessary, boil to reduce it and concentrate the flavour.

2 To finish: if necessary bring the soup to the boil. Stir in the dill and taste again (dill added like this at the last minute adds characteristic freshness of taste). Serve *shchi* with the sour cream in a separate bowl.

Getting Ahead: The more often *shchi* is reheated, the better it is.

On the Side: Dark rye bread, and plenty of it.

In the Glass: Any hearty, robust red wine. When your soup bowl is nearly empty, I'd recommend the Burgundian custom of *faire chabrol*. Add a half glass of wine to the few remaining spoons of soup and savour the waft of alcohol that rises.

BORTSCH

(Serves 8)

This classic winter soup of Eastern Europe and Russia always contains beetroot. Follow the recipe for *Russian Cabbage Soup*, omitting the sauerkraut and mushrooms. Add 900 g/2 lb cooked beetroot, peeled and grated, and 450 g/1 lb tomatoes, peeled, seeded and chopped (page 166), or use canned tomatoes, to the soup with the cabbage. Simmer as directed – the broth will become a rich, glowing red – and season it with a little sugar as well as vinegar, salt and pepper.

Wine Grower's Red Beans with Red Wine

Kidney beans mature shortly before the wine harvest in France – an invitation for grape-pickers to consume vast casseroles of haricots rouges vigneronne, *often in the vineyards. A cheap, fruity local red wine lends gorgeous colour to the beans. The whole piece of bacon with the rind here gives a delicious flavour – you should be able to order it from your butcher. Alternatively, you can omit the bacon and stir a cup of oil-cured black olives into the beans at the end of cooking.*

Serves 3–4 as a main course, 6–8 as a side dish

450 g/1 lb dried red kidney beans

1 onion, studded with 2 cloves

330 g/12 oz piece bacon, with rind

bouquet garni

4 garlic cloves, peeled

salt and pepper

500 ml/16 fl oz robust red wine

medium casserole

GRILLED ESCAROLE, CHICORY, OR RADICCHIO
(Serves 4)
Any of these members of the chicory family do well on the grill, picking up an intriguing tinge of bitterness. I happily eat a whole plate as a first course.

Trim the stems and outer leaves from 1 medium head of escarole, or 3 large heads of chicory, or 3 small heads of radicchio. Cut escarole in eight wedges or chicory or radicchio in quarters, including the stem to hold the pieces together. Toss them with a half cup of olive oil, 3–4 tablespoons balsamic vinegar, salt and pepper. Leave a half hour so the leaves wilt slightly. Light the grill, brush the rack with olive oil and set it quite far (12–15 cm/5–6 in) from the heat. Grill the vegetables, cut-side down, until the top is tender and slightly charred, 5–8 minutes. Turn and continue grilling until the leaves are wilted and tender, 5–8 minutes more.

1 Generously cover the beans with cold water and leave to soak overnight. The next day, drain and rinse them, and then bring them to the boil in fresh water and boil them vigorously for 10 minutes. Drain and rinse again.

2 Heat the oven to 160°C/325°F/Gas Mark 3. Cut the bacon rind off in one piece and put it in the bottom of the casserole dish. Add the beans, onion, bouquet garni, garlic and some pepper and bury the meat in the beans. Pour in enough water to cover the beans generously and add the lid. Bake until the beans are very soft and a few start to burst. This can take 1–3 hours, depending on the age and type of bean and the thickness of the pot, so check occasionally to see how they are doing. If the beans begin to dry, add more water. At the end of cooking, the liquid should have evaporated so that the beans are moist but not soupy. If the liquid is too thin, take the lid off for the last half hour's cooking or, when the beans are done, boil the pot on top of the stove to evaporate the liquid.

3 When the beans are tender, stir in the wine and some salt and pepper. Cover and leave to cool for about an hour, so the beans absorb the wine. Remove the bacon and discard the bouquet garni. Dice the bacon and stir it into the beans. The rind can be discarded or diced and added to the pot.

4 Reheat the beans and, if too much liquid remains, boil to reduce it. Taste, adjust the seasoning and serve.

Shortcut: For a real quickie, use three 420 g cans red kidney beans. Omit the onion and bouquet garni. Dice the bacon and fry it in the casserole until brown. Stir in the garlic and cook for 1 minute. Stir in the beans and wine and simmer, stirring, until the wine is absorbed, 10–15 minutes. Taste for seasoning and serve.

Getting Ahead: Beans with red wine keep well up to three days in the refrigerator, and the more often you heat them, the better they will be.

On the Side: Serve *Winegrower's Red Beans* with roast pork or lamb, or sausages with a side dish of grilled escarole or radicchio (see left).

Mediterranean Fish with Ratatouille

In high summer our garden blooms with a proliferation of courgettes, yellow squash, and misshapen tomatoes, an invitation to freeform versions of ratatouille. To make a full meal I sometimes top mine with fish fillets. This recipe does well with bream (dorade), sea bass and any rich fish such as mackerel or salmon.

Serves 4

675 g/1¹/₂ lb fish fillets

For the ratatouille

1 medium aubergine (about 330 g/12 oz)

2 small courgettes (about 330 g/12 oz)

small bunch of basil (about 30 g/1 oz)

60 ml/2 fl oz olive oil, more for the fish

1 onion, sliced

2 garlic cloves, chopped

1 tablespoon ground coriander

3–4 thyme sprigs

salt and pepper

1 green pepper, cored, seeded and cut in strips

1 red pepper, cored, seeded and cut in strips

450 g/1 lb tomatoes, seeded and chopped

large skillet or deep frying pan with an ovenproof
  handle

1 Heat the oven to 180°C/350°F/Gas Mark 4. Trim the aubergine, cut it in 1.25 cm/¹/₂ in slices, then chunks including the skin. Trim the courgettes, halve them lengthwise, and cut them also in chunks. Strip basil leaves from the stems, roll and shred the leaves, keeping a few sprigs for garnish.

2 Heat half the oil in the skillet and fry the onion until soft but not brown, 3–5 minutes. Stir in the aubergine with the remaining oil, garlic, coriander, thyme sprigs and generous amounts of salt and pepper. Fry, stirring often, for 2 minutes. Stir in the peppers and courgettes and cook for 2 minutes longer. Finally, stir in the tomatoes and basil and cook for 5 minutes more. Taste the ratatouille for seasoning and spread it in an even layer in the skillet.

3 Rinse and dry the fish fillets on paper towels. Sprinkle them with a little olive oil, salt and pepper and lay them on the ratatouille. Bake in the oven until the fish just flakes easily when tested with a fork, 10–12 minutes. The ratatouille should be cooked but still retain some texture. If it seems underdone, transfer the fish fillets to a plate and keep them warm, and cook the ratatouille on top of the stove for a few more minutes. I rather like to serve it directly from the skillet, topped with cheerful sprigs of basil, but by all means transfer it to a serving dish if you prefer, discarding the sprigs of thyme which by now have contributed their flavour.

Getting Ahead: The ratatouille can be prepared up to 12 hours in advance and kept covered in the refrigerator. Add the fish and bake just before serving.

On the Side: Tasty little *Laura's Accordion Potatoes* roasted in olive oil (page 69).

In the Glass: It is not often that I think first of a rosé, the favourite summer wine of Provence, but it would be perfect here.

Moroccan Tajine of Chicken with Aubergine

One of the pleasures of Morocco is the array of dishes cooked in tajines, shallow earthenware baking dishes with a conical lid found nowhere else. The cone traps the cooking juices so the food, often vivid with spice, stays moist and succulent. I've found that a small heavy casserole, just large enough to hold all the ingredients, does very well. The cooking time for chick-peas may seem short but it really does work!

1 Pour boiling water over the chick-peas, covering them generously, and leave them to soak while preparing the aubergines.

2 Trim the aubergines, halve them lengthwise then cut crosswise in 2 cm/³/₄ in slices. Cut the slices in chunks and toss with a tablespoon of salt in a bowl. Leave for 15 minutes to draw out the juices, then rinse with cold water and dry the aubergine on paper towels.

3 Heat 3 tablespoons of the oil in the casserole and add half the aubergine. Fry it, stirring, until browned and quite tender, 8–10 minutes. Take it out, heat more oil and brown the rest. Replace the first batch of aubergine in the casserole and cook gently, stirring, until it is tender, about 10 minutes. Remove it and set aside.

4 Sprinkle the chicken pieces with salt and pepper. Heat the remaining oil and brown the chicken pieces on all sides, allowing 5–7 minutes. Drain the chick-peas and add them to the pan. Mix the ginger, saffron, garlic, 1 teaspoon of salt and water, and pour it over the chicken and peas – they should be just covered. Bring the casserole to the boil, cover and cook over very low heat until the chicken is very tender and falls easily from the bones, 40–50 minutes. Stir from time to time and add more water if the chicken seems dry. If the chick-peas are not tender when the chicken is done, remove the chicken and continue cooking the peas until very tender – cooking time depends very much on the peas.

5 When done, transfer the chicken, chick-peas and sauce to a bowl. Crush the reserved aubergine with a potato masher or fork to a coarse pulp. Stir in 1 tablespoon of the lemon juice and taste for seasoning. Spread the aubergine pulp in the casserole. Put the chicken pieces on top. Stir the remaining lemon juice into the sauce, taste for seasoning and spoon it over the chicken, with the chick-peas. Cover and reheat gently for 8–10 minutes until very hot.

Getting Ahead: The chicken, aubergine and peas can be completely cooked up to two days ahead and refrigerated. Reheat in the casserole over low heat.

In the Glass: Morocco is home to simple, powerful red wines. Take your pick of any similar reds that you know.

Serves 4–6

200 g/7 oz chick-peas

3 medium aubergines (about 1 kg/2¹/₄ lb)

salt and pepper

125 ml/4 fl oz olive oil

1.5 kg/3¹/₂–4 lb chicken, cut in 8 pieces

1 teaspoon ground ginger

large pinch of saffron strands

1 garlic clove, chopped

750 ml/1¹/₄ pints water, more if necessary

juice of 1 lemon

small casserole

Chilean Stew of Chicken, Corn and Pumpkin

This rustic Spanish dish, known as cazuela *(meaning 'casserole'), is a classic one-pot meal, half chicken soup, half stew. Pumpkin, potatoes and corn are a traditional part of* cazuela, *and green vegetables can vary with the season.*

1 Trim any fat from the chicken, leaving some skin for richness. Put the pieces in the pot with the onion, water to cover generously and salt and pepper. Add the lid, bring to the boil and simmer for 30 minutes.

2 Add the potatoes, rice, pumpkin and corn with more water to cover and stir to mix everything together. Cover and continue simmering until the chicken, rice and vegetables are nearly tender, 15–20 minutes longer.

3 Add the green beans and continue simmering until tender, 7–10 minutes. At the end of cooking, the chicken, rice and vegetables should be very tender. Stir the coriander into the broth, taste and adjust the seasoning. Serve the stew in soup bowls with spoons, knives and forks.

Getting Ahead: Keep in the refrigerator for 2–3 days. As you can imagine, it improves when you reheat it. Add the coriander just before serving.

On the Side: Cornbread to absorb the broth – on page 49 there's a recipe for *Anadama Bread*, a hearty cornbread flavoured with molasses.

In the Glass: A glass of good beer, and these days you can probably find one from South America.

Serves 4–6

1 chicken, cut in 8 pieces, or 8 chicken drumsticks

1 onion, sliced

salt and pepper

4 medium potatoes, quartered (about 675 g/1½ lb)

140 g/5 oz rice

450 g/1 lb piece pumpkin, peeled and cut in large chunks

4 corn on the cob, cut across into 3 pieces

170 g/6 oz green beans, trimmed and halved

2 tablespoons chopped coriander

large, heavy-based soup pot

Guinea Fowl with Cabbage and Sausages

My mother once tried to raise guinea fowl, tiresome birds that made a lot of noise and were hard to catch as they persisted in roosting in the trees. So when I moved to France and found guinea fowl ready-prepared in the local market I was delighted. They have much more taste than a chicken and handily replace game birds such as partridge and pheasant. If you cannot find them, use a small chicken instead.

1 Truss the guinea fowl with string (page 166). Heat the oven to 180°C/ 350°F/Gas Mark 4. Quarter the cabbage, discard the core and shred each wedge, cutting across the veins in the leaves. Blanch the cabbage by boiling it in the casserole in salted water, allowing 1 minute after it has come to the boil. Drain the cabbage and set aside.

2 Wipe out the casserole, heat the oil in it and brown the sausages. This will take 2–3 minutes. Take them out, then brown the guinea fowl on all sides. Take it out, add the bacon rashers and fry until starting to brown. Take out half of them. Spread half the cabbage over the remaining bacon and sprinkle with a little salt and pepper. Put the guinea fowl on top, surrounded by the carrots, and cover with the remaining cabbage. Season with salt and pepper and top with the remaining bacon rashers. Pour in the stock and wine. Add the onion and bouquet garni, pushing them well down. Cover and bring to the boil. Simmer in the oven for 1–1¼ hours or until the guinea fowl and carrots are tender. During the last 10 minutes of cooking, add the sausages to the casserole to reheat, pushing them down into the cabbage.

3 When the bird is tender, transfer it to a carving board, and cover it with foil to keep warm. Lift out the sausages, bacon and carrots. Lift out the cabbage with a slotted spoon so the cooking juices are left in the pan. Boil the juices until well flavoured and reduced to about 375 ml/12 fl oz. Discard the onion and bouquet garni from the cabbage and pile it in the centre of a large platter. Either set the guinea fowl on top or cut it into quarters, discarding the backbone, and set the pieces on top. Arrange the sausages, bacon and carrots around the edge of the cabbage. Cover the dish and keep it hot in a low oven while you finish the gravy.

4 Skim off excess fat from the gravy, reheat it, taste and adjust the seasoning. Spoon a little around the cabbage platter and serve the rest separately. Sprinkle the platter with parsley just before serving.

Shortcut: Blanch the cabbage for 5 minutes so it is partly cooked. Cut the guinea fowl in four pieces before browning it. Continue as directed, simmering for only 45–55 minutes until the guinea fowl and carrots are tender.

Getting Ahead: The whole dish can be completely cooked ahead and gently reheated on top of the stove, taking at least 15 minutes so all the contents are hot. I would, however, make the gravy after reheating the bird and cabbage.

On the Side: *Caramelized Tomatoes* (see right) will add a cheerful touch of colour.

In the Glass: A Pinot Noir would be so very good with this recipe, or a simple Beaujolais if your budget is tight.

Serves 4

1.35 kg/3 lb guinea fowl

medium head white cabbage (about 1.35 kg/3 lb)

1½ tablespoons vegetable oil

8 small or 4 medium sausages (about 225 g/8 oz)

8 thickly cut rashers bacon (about 170 g/6 oz)

salt and pepper

6–8 small carrots or 2 large carrots, quartered

500 ml/16 fl oz chicken stock

250 ml/8 fl oz white wine

1 onion, studded with a clove

bouquet garni

2 tablespoons chopped parsley

large casserole

CARAMELIZED TOMATOES

(Serves 4)

I make these tomatoes in generous quantities to serve with almost anything, for example steak, grilled fish or chicken, or a plump veal chop. Set them on a slice of crusty ciabatta bread sprinkled with extra virgin olive oil and you have a champion bruschetta.

Gently heat a large frying pan and sprinkle it with 2 tablespoons sugar. Leave for 2 minutes to melt without stirring, then stir lightly and leave the sugar to cook to a golden caramel. Remove from the heat and at once add 3 tablespoons vinegar, standing back as it can sting your eyes. Stir in 4 tablespoons olive oil and return the pan to the heat, stirring for about a minute until the caramel has dissolved. Let the pan cool slightly, sprinkle with salt and pepper, and add 450 g/1 lb plum tomatoes, halved lengthwise. Tuck 2 rosemary sprigs and 2 bay leaves down among the tomatoes, together with the unpeeled cloves from a whole head of garlic. Cover and cook the tomatoes over a low heat for 15 minutes. Remove the lid and cook for 35–40 minutes, until almost all the liquid has gone.

Duck in Piquant Red-wine Sauce

This charming, rustic recipe comes from Bartolomeo Scappi's Opera, *one of the truly outstanding cookbooks of the Italian renaissance. Everything is simmered together until the duck meat almost falls from the bone. I'm always astonished by the potent, spicy sauce with its underlying sweetness of dried fruits. Scappi does not mention salt, but instead adds ham in much the same way that Italian cooks today season with grated Parmesan cheese. I'd strongly advise cooking the duck ahead – the spices blend and mellow, while the fat that rises to the surface of the sauce during cooking is all the easier to skim after it has solidified in the refrigerator.*

1 Heat the oven to 180°C/350°F/Gas Mark 4. Trim the duck of excess fat and truss it with string (page 166). Combine all the other ingredients in the casserole, stirring to mix them well. Immerse the duck in the pot, breast downwards, pushing it down among the other ingredients. Cover and bring to the boil on top of the stove.

2 Transfer to the oven and bake, occasionally skimming the copious fat that rises to the surface, until the duck is very tender when pierced with a two-pronged fork, 1¹/₂–2 hours. For the last half hour of cooking, remove the lid and set the duck on its back so the skin browns and the sauce thickens. Skim as much fat as possible from the surface of the sauce (this is easier if you remove the bird temporarily). It helps to chill the casserole overnight so the fat rises to the top and solidifies.

3 If necessary, reheat the casserole on top of the stove. Transfer the bird to a platter and spoon the onion and fruits around it, discarding the giblets. If the sauce is thin, boil to reduce it until fairly thick. Taste, adjust the seasoning and serve in a bowl. Discard the trussing strings from the duck just before serving. It can be carved at the table or cut up in the kitchen and laid on top of the fruits and vegetables.

Getting Ahead: You can cook the duck and store it, with the garnish and sauce, ready to reheat in the pot. It keeps for up to three days in the refrigerator, or can be frozen.

On the Side: Polenta, whether freshly cooked or grilled in slices, would be the ideal accompaniment, along with *Braised Leeks* (page 96).

In the Glass: This dish invites an Italian wine, something full-bodied to back up the fruit and spices. For cooking, and indeed for drinking, a Chianti Classico would do well. For a festive occasion, let's be more ambitious – a rich, dark Barolo would be magnificent.

HOMEMADE SPICE POWDER
Make your own spice powder by combining ¹/₂ teaspoon each ground black pepper and ground cinnamon and ¹/₄ teaspoon each ground cloves, grated nutmeg and ground ginger.

Serves 4

1 duck (about 2 kg/4¹/₂ lb) preferably with giblets
4 medium onions, quartered
170 g/6 oz stoned prunes
90 g/3 oz dried cherries or currants
225 g/8 oz cooked lean ham, finely chopped
1 bottle (750 ml) robust red wine
125 ml/4 fl oz red wine vinegar
2 tablespoons dark brown sugar
1 tablespoon chopped sage
2–3 teaspoons homemade spice powder or
  French quatre-épices

large casserole

Provençal Daube of Lamb

Daube is the ultimate one-pot meal of meat, vegetables and broth, marinated in a generous bath of wine. In the old days, a daube was assembled at home, then taken to be baked in the communal village oven so as to save fuel. There are many versions, some with lamb, others with beef, and all moistened with wine of some kind. In winter I like to use a rich, dark red, full of tannin in the style of Provence, with black olives for balance, while summer calls for green olives and the refreshing, softer finish of white wine. I prefer meaty, brine-cured olives for daube. For the lamb, shoulder is always an economical cut, but the stew will be less fatty if you use lean leg meat.

1 Cut the lamb into 3 cm/1^1/$_4$ in cubes, discarding sinew and fat. Stone the olives if you wish. Add oil to the casserole and layer the ingredients on top as follows: lamb, bacon cubes, green and black olives, onions, carrots, tomatoes and garlic. Tie the orange zest, bouquet garni, cinnamon stick, cloves and peppercorns in a piece of muslin and push the bag down into the other ingredients. Pour over the wine. Cover and refrigerate for at least 12 hours and up to a day and a half, stirring occasionally.

2 Heat the oven to 200°C/400°F/Gas Mark 6. Pour enough stock into the casserole to just cover the ingredients and top them with fresh pepper. Add the lid and bring to a simmer in the oven – this will take about half an hour but may vary with the thickness of your casserole.

3 Lower the oven heat to 150°C/300°F/Gas Mark 2 and cook the daube until the lamb is tender enough to crush easily between your finger and thumb, 1^1/$_2$–2 hours. Towards the end of cooking, if the ingredients are swimming in liquid, remove the lid so moisture evaporates.

4 When the meat is done, if the broth is still thin, drain off some of it, boil until concentrated and return it to the pot. Taste the broth and adjust the seasoning – salt may not be needed as the olives and bacon are already salty.

5 To finish, if necessary reheat the daube, stir in the parsley, and check the seasoning once more. Serve from the casserole.

Shortcut: To cut corners, use canned tomatoes, do not bother to stone the olives and, of course, cut down on marinating time.

Getting Ahead: Keep the finished daube a day or two in the refrigerator as the flavour will mellow wonderfully when it is reheated.

On the Side: There's the pleasant choice of adding some small potatoes to the stew, or serve it with one of the breads I suggest on page 49.

In the Glass: A brisk, chilled rosé for the authentic taste of Provence.

GREMOLATA
Purists may shudder, but the Italian gremolata seasoning for *osso buco* is delicious served with daube. To make it, finely chop 2 cloves of garlic, then chop them together with 2–3 tablespoons parsley. Mix in a tablespoon of finely chopped lemon zest. Pass the gremolata at the table for guests to help themselves.

Serves 8

1.35 kg/3 lb boneless lamb leg or shoulder

110 g/4 oz black olives

110 g/4 oz green olives

1 tablespoon olive oil

330 g/12 oz lean smoked bacon, cut in cubes

3 medium onions (about 450 g/1 lb), thinly sliced

3 large carrots (about 450 g/1 lb), thickly sliced

1 kg/2^1/$_4$ lb tomatoes, peeled, seeded, and chopped (page 166)

4–5 garlic cloves, chopped

500 ml/16 fl oz veal stock, more if needed

freshly ground black pepper

salt (optional)

3 tablespoons chopped parsley

For the marinade

pared zest of 1 orange

large bouquet garni

5 cm/2 in cinnamon stick

3 whole cloves

1 teaspoon black peppercorns

500 ml/16 fl oz full-bodied wine

large casserole

Lamb Chops with Onion and Potatoes

Trust the French to improve Irish stew by first browning the chops and onions, then cooking them in stock with sprigs of thyme. (They call this recipe Côtes d'Agneau Champvallon.) *The resulting dish is every French grandmother's pride, a full meal that needs very little attention.*

1 Heat the oven to 180°C/350°F/Gas Mark 4. Trim excess fat from the chops. Heat the oil and half the butter in the skillet and thoroughly brown the chops on both sides over medium-high heat. Remove them and discard all but 2 tablespoons of fat. Add the onions and sauté until well browned, 10–12 minutes. Stir in the garlic, then tip the onions into a large bowl. Add the potatoes, thyme, 2 tablespoons of the parsley, salt and pepper, and stir to mix well.

2 Spread half the potato mixture in the skillet. Add the chops, pushing them down into the potatoes. Cover with the remaining vegetable mixture, arranging the top layer of potatoes in a neat pattern if you like. Pour in enough stock almost to cover the potatoes, then dot them with the remaining butter.

3 Bake the skillet, uncovered, until the potatoes and chops are very tender when pierced with a two-pronged fork, 45–60 minutes. The top of the potatoes should be golden brown and most of the liquid should have been absorbed so don't hesitate to cook for a few more minutes. Crispy brown potatoes and rich gravy are important. Sprinkle the dish with the remaining parsley and serve in the skillet.

Getting Ahead: This can be cooked up to two days ahead and stored in the refrigerator, provided the pan you use is non-metallic. Reheat the dish on top of the stove.

In the Glass: This dish goes well with red wine or beer, whichever is your pleasure.

Serves 4

4 lamb chops with bone (about 900 g/2 lb)
1 tablespoon vegetable oil
45 g/1$\frac{1}{2}$ oz butter
2 large onions, thinly sliced
1 garlic clove, chopped
6 potatoes, thinly sliced (about 900 g/2 lb)
small bunch of fresh thyme (about 15 g/$\frac{1}{2}$ oz)
3–4 tablespoons chopped parsley
salt and pepper
500 ml/16 fl oz veal stock (page 166), more if
  needed

large skillet or shallow flameproof casserole

Emily's Braised Beef with Carrots

To call this recipe boiled beef would be a travesty, a betrayal of my childhood mentor, Emily, who reigned in the kitchen. Her weekday beef with carrots, gently baked in the oven beside the open fire, was infinitely preferable to my mind to the roast sirloin reserved for Sundays. It was only later that I discovered her beef contained a fair measure of red wine. It was later, too, that I realized that another reason for Emily's success was the beef. Emily favoured a tough, gelatinous cut that took many hours to cook and yielded a rich, glossy sauce. In the US, chuck roast would have been her choice, and in England it was silverside.

1 Heat the oven to 160°C/325°F/Gas Mark 3. Heat 2 tablespoons of the oil in the casserole and brown the beef on all sides over medium heat, taking 8–10 minutes to colour it well. Remove it, add the bacon and cook until the fat runs. Add the onions and fry, stirring, until the bacon and onions are browned, 5–7 minutes. Remove them also.

2 Heat the remaining oil and fry the carrots and celery for 2–3 minutes. Stir in the onions and bacon and then set the beef on top, pushing it down into the vegetables. Add the wine, bring to the boil and simmer for about 5 minutes. Add the stock, bouquet garni and a little salt and pepper. Cover and bring the liquid to the boil.

3 Transfer the casserole to the oven and cook for about 1 1/2 hours. At this point, turn the meat to keep it moist; if the pan seems dry, add more stock. Continue cooking until the beef is tender and the vegetables are very soft, 1/2–1 hour more, a total time of 2–2 1/2 hours.

4 Remove the beef and vegetables, cover them with foil and keep them warm. Discard the bouquet garni. The cooking juices should have reduced to a dark gravy so, if necessary, continue boiling until they are concentrated.

5 Make the kneaded butter for thickening: crush the butter with a fork and work in the flour to a smooth paste. Drop small pieces of kneaded butter into the simmering gravy, whisking constantly so it thickens evenly. Stir in the chopped thyme and simmer for 1 minute. Taste, adjust the seasoning and keep the gravy warm.

6 Discard the string from the beef and carve it in 1.25 cm/1/2 in slices; arrange them, overlapping, on a large serving dish and pile the vegetables alongside. Moisten the meat with a little gravy and serve the rest separately.

Serves 6–8

3 tablespoons vegetable oil

1.35 kg/3 lb piece of stewing beef, rolled and tied

200 g/7 oz bacon, diced

450 g/1 lb onions, cut into wedges

1 kg/2 1/4 lb carrots, thickly sliced

3 celery sticks, thickly sliced

500 ml/16 fl oz red wine

300 ml/10 fl oz brown stock or chicken stock (page 165), more if needed

bouquet garni

salt and pepper

1 tablespoon chopped fresh thyme (to finish)

For the kneaded butter

30 g/1 oz butter, softened

2 tablespoons flour

large casserole

Shortcut: Cut the beef in 4 cm/1 1/2 in cubes, brown the cubes and continue as directed. You'll reduce the braising time to 1 1/2 hours.

Getting Ahead: Like so many slow-cooked dishes, *Beef with Carrots* reheats superbly. Keep it in the refrigerator for up to three days and reheat it gently on top of the stove.

On the Side: Mashed potatoes are perfect.

In the Glass: More of the red wine that proves so beneficial in the stew, if possible a Cabernet Sauvignon or a Bordeaux-style blend.

Portuguese Pork with Clams

One of the world's most successful meat and shellfish combinations comes from Portugal, where sautéed pork is enlivened with the little Venus clams familiar in Italian spaghetti alla vongole. *Any small clam can be substituted. If you like food hot, sprinkle a few drops of Tabasco on the stew just before serving.*

1 Wash the clams, discarding any which do not close when tapped on the work surface. Trim any sinew or fat from the tenderloin and cut it into 2.5 cm/1 in cubes. Mix the paprika, flour and pepper and toss the pork cubes until well coated. Do not season with salt as the clams may be salty.

2 Heat half the olive oil in the sauté or frying pan, add the pork and sauté over medium heat until browned on all sides for 5–7 minutes, stirring often. The meat should not be crowded, so you may need to brown it in two batches. Remove it and set aside.

3 Heat the remaining oil in the pan and fry the onion until starting to brown. Stir in the pork with the garlic, water, tomato purée if using, bay leaves and pepper. Cover and cook gently until the pork is almost tender, 8–10 minutes.

4 Set the clams on top, cover the pan and keep cooking until the clams just open, 5–7 minutes. Discard any that do not open. Do not overcook the clams or they will be tough.

On the Side: You'll have a satisfying meal if you add some cooked canned white or red kidney beans (please do not compromise with ordinary baked beans). They can be heated in the same pot: when the pork is almost tender, stir in the cooked beans and heat until very hot, 4–5 minutes. Add the clams and continue as directed.

In the Glass: A light refreshing white wine, on the lines of Portuguese Vinho Verde.

Serves 4

3 litres/5 pints/about 30 small clams

675 g/1¹/₂ lb pork tenderloin

1 tablespoon paprika

1 tablespoon flour

salt and pepper

3 tablespoons olive oil

1 onion, chopped

3–4 garlic cloves, crushed

2 tablespoons water

2 tablespoons tomato purée (optional)

2 bay leaves

large sauté pan or deep frying pan

The world is divided in two halves: pastry-makers whose hands by nature are chilly and bread-makers with warm hands like me. I love to launch myself into warm, yeasty dough, and offbeat breads that use different grains are my forte. What is the point of making the same loaves that you can perfectly well buy at a good bakery?

Anadama Bread (Makes 1 large freeform loaf)

Anadama is a traditional colonial bread from New England. Hearsay has it that a farmer was cursing his lazy wife, who persisted in serving him bland cornmeal mush. He worked in flour, yeast and molasses to make bread, muttering 'Anna, damn 'er' all the while.

7 g/^{1}/$_4$ oz active dry yeast
1 teaspoon sugar
300 ml/10 fl oz warm water
2 tablespoons vegetable oil
110 g/4 oz dark molasses
1 tablespoon salt
200 g/7 oz yellow cornmeal
390 g/14 oz unbleached strong white flour,
    more if needed

electric mixer fitted with dough hook

Sprinkle the yeast and sugar over 60 ml/2 fl oz warm water in the bowl of the mixer. Leave for 5 minutes until the yeast is dissolved and starts to bubble. Stir the remaining water, oil, molasses and salt in a bowl and mix it into the yeast. Add the cornmeal and beat until mixed. Add the flour gradually, beating vigorously; the dough will be very sticky.

Knead the dough for 3–4 minutes, little by little adding enough flour to make a smooth dough that is springy to the touch. Shape into a ball, put it in an oiled bowl, and turn it to coat the surface. Cover it and let rise in a warm, draught-free place until doubled in bulk, 1–1^1/$_4$ hours.

Oil a baking sheet and sprinkle it generously with cornmeal. Turn the dough on to a floured work surface and shape into one round loaf, as high and plump as possible. Be careful not to overwork the dough as it may collapse. Transfer the loaf to the baking sheet and sprinkle with more cornmeal. Leave to rise uncovered in a warm place until almost doubled in bulk, 30–45 minutes. Heat the oven to 220°C/425°F/Gas Mark 7.

Using a razor blade or the point of a sharp knife, slash the top of the loaf in a wide crosshatch pattern. Bake it for 10 minutes before lowering the heat to 180°C/ 350°F/Gas Mark 4. Continue baking until the loaf is well browned and sounds hollow when tapped on the bottom, 30–35 minutes longer. Transfer to a rack to cool.

Cracked Wheat Bread (Makes 2 medium loaves)

Most breads are raised twice, once after kneading, and again after shaping. Cracked wheat bread, however, is kneaded very lightly and raised only once, in the pan, and so is quick to make. Unlike more conventional breads it does not rise much in the oven. Vary the texture by using fine- or medium-grain cracked wheat.

butter for the tins
20 g/^{3}/$_4$ oz dry active yeast
750 ml/1^1/$_4$ pints lukewarm water, more if needed
390 g/14 oz unbleached strong white flour, more for
    sprinkling
250 g/9 oz fine or medium cracked wheat
2 teaspoons salt

2 medium loaf tins (1.25-litre/2^1/$_4$-pint capacity each)

Butter the loaf tins. Sprinkle the yeast over 125 ml/ 4 fl oz of the water and leave it for 5 minutes or until dissolved. Mix the flour and cracked wheat in a bowl with the salt. Make a well in the centre with your hand and add the dissolved yeast, with the remaining water. Mix with your hands to form a dough – it should be quite sticky. Knead in the bowl for 2 minutes – this is long enough as the dough should not become elastic.

Turn the dough on to a floured work surface and divide it in half. Pat each half to a rectangle 20 cm/8 in wide and roll it to a cylinder. Seal the seam and set the dough seam-side down in a loaf tin. Repeat with the other piece of dough. Leave the loaves to rise in a warm place until the tins are full, 35–45 minutes. Heat the oven to 190°C/375°F/Gas Mark 5.

If you like a floury top, sprinkle the loaves with a little flour. Finally, bake them low down in the oven (plenty of bottom heat helps them rise) until brown and the base sounds hollow when tapped, 35–45 minutes. Turn the loaves on to a rack to cool.

TIPS ON BREAD

Storing bread: Rich breads containing plenty of eggs or fat keep well for 2–3 days in an airtight container, though they are best warmed or toasted for serving. Plainer breads, however, either lose their attractive crispness or dry out, sometimes within a few hours. It helps to wrap them in a cloth (rather than a plastic bag) so they remain gently moist. You can buy bread bins that will maintain the right humidity for storage. After a day or so, toast is the happiest end for plain breads.

Freezing bread: Many breads freeze well, and this includes both the recipes here. After defrosting, I usually freshen a loaf by warming it in a low oven just before serving. Alternatively, slice breads after defrosting, and toast the slices.

Just the other day I was talking to a culinary student who described how hard she found it to plan for a family reunion. Her sister avoided high-cholesterol foods, her brother was vegetarian and so it went on. Eventually she found a dish to please everyone. True enough, I thought, there are dishes that have universal appeal like pancakes and macaroni cheese, friendly dishes that are easy to enjoy.

So this chapter is full of old favourites like meatballs and pasta pie. Some of the recipes are an invitation for children to join in the action – I think particularly of *Stromboli*, a version of pizza where the dough is shaped with filling like a jam roly-poly. In the dessert chapters you'll find more ideas for pulling the family into the kitchen, such as cherries dipped in chocolate and *California Cornmeal Cake*, mixed in the processor.

It can be surprising what children like to eat – ours started, aged five and seven, with a passion for mussels in the shell and worked up to snails and squid. In the kitchen Simon made the vinaigrette dressing, while Emma baked a mean apple crumble. We all loved roast pork and fish pie, and we still do. Never mind that Emma continues to reject our garden Brussels sprouts.

Our children now are long grown up, and their favourite dishes have changed with them. The breakfast pancakes, bacon and maple syrup of school weekends have become little blini made with buckwheat flour and served with smoked salmon and crème fraîche. An acceptance of a bit of spice in pot roast has become a full blown devotion to Indian curry, hot, with all the trimmings. So please don't be surprised that I include *Spicy Lamb Hotpot* and *Chicken Satay* in family fare. Kids grow up, they travel and bring back with them a taste for exotic dishes and curious combinations. It is now Emma who introduces me to the dishes she discovered in Mexico. She has me shopping for tortillas, and adding a suspicion of dark chocolate to my red-wine sauce, in echo of *mole*. The dishes on our family table are an ongoing adventure, so why not join us!

Family Fare

Count Rocca's Minestrone

Carlo Maria Rocca was a celebrated figure on the Venetian scene, known for his hospitality and the authentic country recipes that he prepared himself. Minestrone, for me, had always been a cheerful broth of vegetables with a bit of macaroni and dried beans, until I tasted Carlo Maria's amazing vegetable stew, flavoured with rinds of Parmesan cheese and simmered for 3–4 hours to an astonishing intensity. Please don't be tempted to thin his minestrone to a pourable soup – it should be so thick that 'a spoon stands up in it'. Basil and grated Parmesan cheese are added just before serving.

Serves 8–10

60 ml/2 fl oz olive oil

2 medium onions, chopped

1 medium carrot, chopped

2 celery sticks, chopped

2 medium courgettes, chopped with the skin

20–25 green beans, trimmed and cut in
  2 cm/3/4 in sticks

2 tomatoes, peeled, seeded and chopped
  (page 166)

1 potato, peeled and cut in medium dice

3–4 leaves Savoy cabbage or kale, finely
  shredded

300 g/11 oz frozen green peas

200 g/7 oz dried white kidney beans

60 g/2 oz prosciutto, diced (optional)

salt and pepper

2–3 pieces of rind from Parmesan cheese
  (optional)

500 ml/16 fl oz water, more if needed

To finish the soup

bunch of basil

75 g/2½ oz grated Parmesan cheese

60 ml/2 fl oz extra virgin olive oil, more for
  serving

1 Heat the oven to 160°C/325°F/Gas Mark 3, if you don't want to cook the soup on the stove. Heat the oil in a soup pot, add the onions and fry gently until very tender but not browned, 5–7 minutes. Stir in the carrot, celery, courgettes, green beans, tomatoes, potato, cabbage or kale, peas, beans and prosciutto, if using. Add a little salt and plenty of pepper and tuck in the cheese rinds, if using. Add the water to generate steam when cooking begins.

2 Cover the pot and cook over very low heat, or in the oven, stirring occasionally, until the vegetables are very tender and the flavour is concentrated, 3–4 hours. If the vegetables seem dry, add more water. The minestrone should be the consistency of soft risotto. Discard the Parmesan rinds.

3 To finish: reheat the soup. Coarsely shred leaves from the basil, reserving sprigs for decoration. Stir the shredded basil, grated Parmesan and olive oil into the minestrone. Taste and adjust the seasoning. Serve the soup in bowls, topped with a basil sprig. If you like, pass a bottle of your favourite virgin olive oil to drizzle on top.

Shortcut: Use fewer vegetables and more of them, always including some roots, greens, beans and tomatoes (you could use a small can of chopped tomatoes).

Getting Ahead: Quantities for this minestrone are generous and it can be kept in the refrigerator for up to two days. The flavour mellows, and I would add a little water so it does not stick when you reheat it on top of the stove.

On the Side: Italian ciabatta bread.

In the Glass: Let's go Italian all the way, with generous quantities of dry white Soave or a more full-bodied Bardolino, both from the Veneto.

Fish Pie in a Baked Potato

Shepherd's pie has travelled worldwide, but traditional English fish pie is a surprisingly well kept secret. We had it regularly in my childhood, in the days when cod was cheap. Big flakes of fish were served in a white sauce, generously perfumed with nutmeg and chopped parsley, with hard-boiled eggs to make it go further, plus a browned topping of mashed potato. I always had seconds. Here's a contemporary take on the theme.

Serves 4

4 large baking potatoes (about 900 g/2 lb)

salt and pepper

170 g/6 oz skinless cod or other white fish fillets, coarsely chopped

60 g/2 oz cooked, peeled medium prawns, halved lengthwise

1 hard-boiled egg, coarsely chopped

60 g/2 oz melted butter

For the parsley sauce

375 ml/12 fl oz milk

slice of onion

6 peppercorns

1 bay leaf

2 tablespoons chopped parsley (reserve the stems)

30 g/1 oz butter

2 tablespoons flour

grated nutmeg

1 Heat the oven to 190°C/375°F/Gas Mark 5. Wash the potatoes and rub them with salt while still damp, so the salt sticks and will make the skin more crisp. Prick them with a fork and bake them in the oven until tender when pierced with a skewer, 1–1¹/₄ hours.

2 Scald the milk in a wide, shallow pan with the onion, peppercorns, bay leaf, parsley stems and a little salt and pepper, cover and leave over low heat to infuse, about 10 minutes. Add the fish to the milk and simmer until it flakes easily, 2–3 minutes. Transfer the fish to a plate, strain and reserve the milk.

3 For the filling, first make the sauce: melt the butter in a saucepan, whisk in the flour and cook for a few moments. Add the reserved milk and bring the sauce to the boil, whisking constantly until it thickens. Let it simmer for 1 minute, take from the heat and stir in the chopped parsley. Season it to taste with nutmeg, salt and pepper. Flake the fish with a fork, discarding any bones, and stir it into the sauce, with the prawns and egg. Taste and adjust the seasoning.

4 When the potatoes are done, let them cool slightly, then cut a sliver off the top to make a lid and discard it. Scoop the potato pulp into a bowl, leaving a shell of cooked potato and skin. Scoop out as much pulp as you can so there's maximum room for the filling. Fill the shell with the fish mixture. Using a potato masher or fork, lightly crush the potato pulp with the melted butter, salt and pepper and spread it on the filling. Set the potatoes in an oiled baking dish and bake in the oven until brown, 20–25 minutes – they should start to bubble and sizzle. (If potato is left over, spread it in a separate dish and bake it with the potatoes.) Serve very hot.

Shortcut: Substitute ready-made tartlet shells for the baked potato, and fill them with the fish and prawn mixture.

Getting Ahead: Prepare and fill the potatoes up to 24 hours ahead and keep them covered in the refrigerator. Reheat them at 180°C/350°F/Gas Mark 4 until very hot and browned, 35–45 minutes.

On the Side: Halve some tomatoes and sprinkle them with a mixture of breadcrumbs, chopped parsley and salt and pepper, moistened with olive oil. Bake them in the oven beside the potatoes.

In the Glass: For this family dish I would propose a glass of apple juice, with cider for the adults.

Chicken Satay with Peanut Sauce

In south-east Asia, vendors are well aware that it's the sizzle and smell of outdoor snacks like these satays that make them so appealing. They are equally good made with pork fillet.

1 Cut each chicken breast into 6–8 strips, about 1 cm/³/₈ in thick. (When cut in strips they absorb more marinade.) For the marinade: stir together all the ingredients in a bowl, add the chicken strips and mix well. Cover and marinate in the refrigerator for 1–3 hours. At the same time, fill a shallow tray with water and soak the skewers so they do not splinter or burn during cooking.

2 To finish: heat the barbecue or grill. Drain the skewers and spear the chicken on each one, pleating the strips to and fro to form a zigzag pattern. They slip about a bit, so you'll need to persevere! Brush the rack with oil and add the chicken skewers. Grill the satays about 5–7.5 cm/2–3 in from the heat until brown, 2–3 minutes, then turn and brown the other side, 2–3 minutes longer – they should be slightly charred, but still moist inside.

Shortcut: Reduce the marinating time to just a few minutes. When grilling the satays, baste them often with marinade.

Getting Ahead: Satays are just as good at room temperature so by all means cook them an hour or two ahead. Do not, however, refrigerate them or they will lose their fragrance.

On the Side: *Peanut Sauce* (see below) is the traditional accompaniment for satays, but they are delicious plain too with a tomato or cucumber salad.

In the Glass: A long, cool glass of iced tea, fresh lemonade, or beer.

Serves 4–6

4 boneless, skinless chicken breasts
  (about 550 g/1¹/₄ lb)

For the marinade

2 lemon grass stems or 2 shallots, chopped

2 garlic cloves, chopped

1.25 cm/¹/₂ in piece of fresh root ginger, finely
  chopped

2 teaspoons Chinese five-spice powder

2 tablespoons soy sauce

2 tablespoons vegetable oil

1 tablespoon honey

12 wooden skewers
barbecue or grill

PEANUT SAUCE
(Makes about 375 ml/12 fl oz, serves 4–6)
Heat a tablespoon of vegetable oil in a frying pan and fry 170 g/6 oz dry-roasted peanuts, stirring until brown, 2–3 minutes. Put them in a processor with ¹/₂ an onion, cut in pieces, 1 garlic clove, 1 teaspoon ground ginger, 1 tablespoon lemon juice, 1 teaspoon sugar and ¹/₂ teaspoon dried chilli pepper flakes. Purée the mixture until very smooth. With the blades running, pour about 250 ml/8 fl oz hot water down the feed tube, enough to make a pourable sauce. Taste, adjust the seasoning and transfer to a saucepan. Heat it until hand-hot and serve in individual dishes for dipping.

Spicy Lamb Hotpot

The sauce for this classic Indian dish is thickened with a purée of dried peas, which also marries the spices and soothes the heat of chilli. Just how much heat to generate – fiery, mild or even none at all – is entirely your choice.

Serves 6

60 g/2 oz dried split yellow peas

300 ml/10 fl oz water

1 kg/2¼ lb boneless shoulder of lamb

2–3 tablespoons vegetable oil

4 onions, chopped (about 450 g/1 lb)

2 teaspoons ground ginger

2 teaspoons ground cinnamon

½ teaspoon ground cloves

½ teaspoon dried chilli pepper flakes, less or
 more to taste

seeds of 1 cardamom pod

salt and pepper

750 ml/1¼ pints chicken stock, or water, more
 if needed

pinch of saffron strands (optional)

To finish the sauce

1 tablespoon each of fresh lemon juice and
 wine vinegar

generous handful of chopped coriander

1 Put the peas in a small pan with the water, cover and simmer for ³/₄–1 hour, until very tender. Stir now and then, and add more water if the peas seem dry. When tender, purée the peas and their cooking water in a blender, or push them through a sieve.

2 Meanwhile heat the oven to 160°C/325°F/Gas Mark 3. (The hotpot can also be simmered on top of the stove, but then it needs more attention as it can stick on the bottom.) Trim any sinew and most of the fat from the lamb and cut it into 4 cm/1½ in cubes. Heat the oil in a medium casserole and brown a few pieces of the lamb over high heat. Remove them, then brown the rest and remove them also. Add the onions and fry over medium heat until soft and starting to brown, 5–7 minutes. Stir in the ginger, cinnamon, cloves, chilli, cardamom seeds, salt and pepper. Fry over low heat, stirring constantly, for 1–2 minutes until the spices are very fragrant.

3 Stir in the stock or water and bring to the boil. Stir in the meat, pushing it down into the liquid; add more stock or water if needed to cover the meat completely. Cover the casserole, bring to the boil, and cook in the oven for 1 hour, stirring occasionally. Add more water if the pan seems dry.

4 Stir in the pea purée and saffron, if using. Cook for ½–1 hour more, until the meat is very tender. At the end of cooking the sauce should be rich and thick; if it seems thin, take off the lid and boil to thicken it. Stir in the lemon juice and vinegar – this traditional last-minute addition gives a great boost to the sauce. Taste and adjust the seasoning. Serve the hotpot in the cooking pot, sprinkled with coriander.

On the Side: Serve with fragrant boiled basmati rice, Indian-style chutney, and *Cucumber Raita* (see below).

In the Glass: Beer and lager go best with curry, I think.

CUCUMBER RAITA

(Makes 500 ml/16 fl oz, serves 4–6)

Yoghurt, the lead ingredient in raita, is an instant antidote to the heat of chilli, while cucumber adds crunch. I'm fond of raita with other dishes, too, such as *Moroccan Tabbouleh* (page 17) and *Chicken Satay* (page 54), and it also makes a pleasant dip with *Pitta Chips* (page 87) as a first course.

  Peel a medium cucumber, cut it in half lengthwise and scoop out the seeds with a teaspoon. Coarsely grate the halves, sprinkle lightly with salt and leave in a strainer about an hour to draw out the juices. Press to extract the juices and mix the cucumber in a bowl with a medium tomato, seeded and chopped, ½ a small onion, grated, 250 ml/8 fl oz natural yoghurt, and more salt if needed. Raita keeps well for up to a day. Shortly before serving, stir in 2 tablespoons chopped coriander or parsley.

Simon's Meatballs

*When the children were in their early teens, we took a vacation in Scandinavia. All was a success – the sun, the long days, the great outdoors – except for the food, best described as limited. Only the meatballs (*frikadeller*) reached the high family standards, and our son, Simon, has had a fondness for them ever since. If you can't get the traditional veal, use all minced pork.*

1 Pull the bread into pieces and soak it in the milk. Put the minced pork and veal in a processor and purée them, using the pulse button and working as lightly as possible.
2 Add the onion, egg yolks, spices and salt and pepper and pulse just until mixed. Squeeze the excess liquid from the soaked bread, pull it apart into crumbs and add to the meat mixture. Pulse again, adding 1–2 tablespoons more milk if the mixture is dry. Brown a small piece of mixture in a frying pan and taste it, adding more salt and pepper if needed. Chill the mixture for at least 30 minutes, so it is firm and easy to handle. The meatball mixture can also be made by hand, beating in the other ingredients with a wooden spoon.
3 Dampen a chopping board and roll the meat mixture to a loose cylinder about 30 cm/12 in long. Cut it in 12 portions. Dip your hands in a bowl of cold water and roll the meat into even balls.
4 Heat the butter in a frying pan until the spluttering stops. Add the meatballs and sauté them over medium heat until they are evenly browned, turning them often, 6–8 minutes. Turn down the heat, cover the pan and continue cooking until the beads of juice running from the meatballs are clear, not pink, 7–10 minutes. Transfer them to a serving dish and keep warm.
5 Add the mushrooms with lemon juice, salt and pepper. Fry over medium heat, stirring, until the mushrooms are tender, 3–5 minutes. Stir in the dill or parsley, taste, adjust the seasoning and spoon over the *frikadeller*.

Getting Ahead: The meatballs can be kept in the refrigerator for a day. Reheat them gently or they will be tough.

On the Side: The traditional Scandinavian accompaniment of boiled potatoes, pickled beetroot and cucumber salad has never been for us. We turn to lots of mashed potato.

In the Glass: More good milk, or a glass of light Scandinavian beer.

Serves 4

2 slices white bread
250 ml/8 fl oz milk, more if needed
330 g/12 oz minced lean pork
330 g/12 oz minced lean veal
1 small onion, grated
2 egg yolks
1/4 teaspoon grated nutmeg
1/4 teaspoon ground allspice
1 teaspoon salt, more to taste
1/4 teaspoon ground pepper, more to taste
45 g/1 1/2 oz butter
225 g/8 oz button mushrooms, thinly sliced
squeeze of lemon juice
2 tablespoons chopped dill or parsley

food processor, optional

Bulgarian Lamb and Vegetable Stew

Kavarma is a national dish in Bulgaria, a stew that can be made with any meat – beef, lamb, pork, even with chicken. 'Many leeks,' instructs Bulgarian-born Chef Nikolay Stoianov, 'mushroom, tomato, garlic, and chubritsa of course.' Chubritsa is a variety of mint that grows wild on the mountains, though the flavour more closely resembles oregano or savory. The stew is often baked in individual, boat-shaped dishes called gondolas, and one day I was served kavarma in a small water pitcher, the perfect shape for retaining the cooking juices. When I asked about an accompaniment of potatoes, Nikolay shook his head emphatically. 'No, no,' he said, 'it comes alone.'

1 Heat the oven to 200°C/400°F/Gas Mark 6. Cut the lamb in 2.5 cm/1 in cubes, discarding skin and fat. Heat the oil in a casserole and brown pieces of lamb on all sides, working in 2–3 batches. Remove it and add the leeks, onions, garlic, salt and pepper. Fry over medium heat, stirring often, until the vegetables are wilted. Stir in the meat and add water to just cover. Top with the tomatoes, mushrooms, oregano or savory, salt and pepper. Stir together and bring the stew to the boil.

2 Cook it, uncovered, in the oven for 30 minutes. Stir again, cover, and continue cooking until the lamb and vegetables are very tender, 1–1¹/₂ hours longer. Taste and adjust the seasoning. Sprinkle the stew with the parsley just before serving.

Getting Ahead: The stew can be cooked up to two days ahead and kept in the refrigerator, or frozen. Reheat it on top of the stove and then add the parsley.

On the Side: Some dark, crusty bread.

In the Glass: Bulgaria lays claim to being the birthplace of winemaking, so try a glass of a famous red Bulgarian wine, such as a Cabernet Sauvignon or Merlot, with this stew. A cold beer is a refreshing alternative.

Serves 4–6

900 g/2 lb boneless leg or shoulder of lamb

2 tablespoons vegetable oil

450 g/1 lb leeks, sliced including some of the green tops

2 onions, sliced

4 garlic cloves, chopped

salt and pepper

330 g/12 oz tomatoes, seeded and chopped

225 g/8 oz mushrooms, sliced

3–4 tablespoons chopped oregano or savory

2–3 tablespoons chopped parsley

Aubergine Parmigiana

Aubergine Parmigiana is overdue for a revival, but forget those dowdy restaurant concoctions of a generation ago. Home-made Parmigiana is light and wonderfully intense in flavour as the aubergine slices are baked with a brushing of oil rather than fried, and the tomatoes are only lightly cooked to a purée.

Serves 6

3 medium aubergines (about 900 g/2 lb)
about 175 ml/6 fl oz olive oil for brushing,
   more if needed
125 g/4¹/₂ oz Parmesan cheese, grated
225 g/8 oz mozzarella cheese, sliced

For the tomato purée

1.35 kg/3 lb plum tomatoes
2 tablespoons oil
salt and pepper
small bunch of basil (about 30 g/1 oz)

20 cm/8 in square baking dish

1 Heat the oven to 190°C/375°F/Gas Mark 5. Trim the aubergines and cut them in 1 cm/³/₈ in slices. Brush two baking sheets generously with oil, add the aubergine rounds and brush them also. Bake them in the oven until the slices are brown underneath, 12–15 minutes. Turn them, brush again with oil and brown the other side, 7–10 minutes longer.
2 Meanwhile make the tomato purée: halve the tomatoes crosswise and squeeze out the seeds (if you like, sieve the seeds and add the juice to the purée). Coarsely chop them, discarding the cores. Heat the oil in a skillet or shallow saucepan and add the tomatoes with salt and pepper. Cook them, stirring often, for 20–25 minutes to form a purée that just falls easily from the spoon. Chop the basil leaves, reserving sprigs for decoration. Stir the leaves into the tomato sauce, taste and adjust the seasoning.
3 Oil the baking dish and arrange a third of the aubergine slices in it. Sprinkle with a third of the Parmesan cheese and add a layer of half the mozzarella; top with half the tomato sauce. Continue with layers of aubergine, cheese and tomato, ending with a layer of aubergine sprinkled with Parmesan cheese. Drizzle with a little oil.
4 Bake in the oven until very hot, browned, and the mozzarella cheese has melted, 25–35 minutes. Decorate with basil sprigs when serving.

Shortcut: In winter I substitute canned plum tomatoes as fresh ones are so insipid.

Getting Ahead: Prepare *Aubergine Parmigiana* up to two days ahead and refrigerate it, or freeze it for up to three months. Bake it just before serving.

On the Side: A constant supply of hot garlic bread is ideal.

In the Glass: For this traditional recipe with a new look, I suggest a classic – Chianti. Many Chianti growers have changed their style, too, in favour of lighter table wines.

Canadian Buckwheat Pancakes with Bacon and Maple Syrup

This recipe for Canadian buckwheat pancakes – or ployes (pronounced 'ploys') – comes from Laura Calder, who was raised in rural New Brunswick, on Canada's east coast. 'My grandparents ate ployes for supper four nights a week!' she says. Ployes should be quite thin, thinner than a breakfast pancake, and only one side is browned, leaving a tender surface to absorb the topping. Tiny ones make excellent canapés.

1 For the batter: sift the buckwheat and white flours into a bowl with the baking powder and salt. Make a well in the centre and add half the water. Stir with a whisk to form a smooth paste. Bring the remaining water to the boil and stir it into the batter. It should be the consistency of double cream.
2 Fry the bacon on a griddle or skillet and then drain on paper towels. Discard all but a tablespoon of fat. Heat until a few drops of water splutter when dropped on the hot surface; then turn the heat down quite low. Using a pitcher or ladle, pour in 3–4 10 cm/4 in pancakes. Cook over medium heat until the upper surfaces of the ployes are firm and the undersides are golden brown, 2–3 minutes. (Laura often flips and browns the upper surface too, but that is not traditional.) Transfer the ployes to a plate, piling them on top of each other to keep warm and moist. They should be about 3 mm/1/8 in thick; if too thick, add more boiling water to the batter before cooking the next batch.
3 Serve the pancakes warm with the bacon, and maple syrup on the side.

Getting Ahead: Your pancakes will be even lighter if the batter is made an hour or so in advance; keep it covered at room temperature.

On the Side: Ployes accompany savoury dishes such as pea soup or pork and beans, and are also good with smoked salmon and sour cream and, of course, with caviar. I call them easy blini, a child's play version of the Russian pancakes.

In the Glass: A brunch of ployes needs a mug of hot coffee. For supper, how about a glass of cold milk?

Makes 20–24 10 cm/4 in ployes, to serve 6

125 g/4 1/2 oz buckwheat flour
75 g/2 1/2 oz unbleached plain white flour
1 tablespoon baking powder
1/2 teaspoon salt
425 ml/14 fl oz water, more if needed
1 lb/450 g streaky bacon, thinly sliced
250 ml/8 fl oz maple syrup

Goats' Cheese Gougère

Gougères are the savoury version of cream puffs, flavoured with cheese, and we love them so much at home that I've developed several versions over the years. This one is flat, resembling a light pizza, and you can add any herb to the topping and a bit of garlic, too, if you like.

Serves 6

125 g/4¹/₂ oz Gruyère cheese

125 g/4¹/₂ oz unbleached plain white flour

175 ml/6 fl oz milk

¹/₂ teaspoon salt

75 g/2¹/₂ oz unsalted butter, cut in pieces

4 eggs

For the topping

125 g/4¹/₂ oz goats' cheese (about ³/₄ log)

1 tablespoon chopped thyme, rosemary, sage or tarragon

1 garlic clove, crushed (optional)

1 tablespoon olive oil (for brushing), more for the pan

25–28 cm/10–11 in tart tin with removable base (optional)

1 Heat the oven to 190°C/375°F/Gas Mark 5. Brush the tart tin with oil. Cut the Gruyère cheese in small dice and the goats' cheese in 6–8 slices.

2 For the choux pastry: sift the flour on to a sheet of paper. In a small saucepan heat the milk, salt and butter until the butter is melted. Bring to the boil, take from the heat and immediately add all the flour. Beat vigorously with a wooden spoon for a few moments until the mixture pulls away from the sides of the pan to form a ball. Beat for ¹/₂–1 minute over low heat to dry the dough slightly, just until it starts to stick to the base of the pan. Take the dough from the heat and let it cool 2–3 minutes.

3 Beat the eggs one by one into the dough, using the wooden spoon or a hand-held electric mixer. Adding just the right amount of egg is the key to choux pastry, so break the last egg into a small bowl, whisk it with a fork to mix, and add it a little at a time – you may not need all of it. At the end the dough will be shiny and should just fall from the spoon. Beat in the diced Gruyère cheese.

4 Spread the dough evenly in the tart tin, using the back of a spoon (for a more rustic effect, simply spread the dough in a round on an oiled baking sheet). Sprinkle with the herbs, and garlic if using, leaving a 2 cm/³/₄ in border of dough. Top the herbs with rounds of goats' cheese – the dough will show between them. Brush the cheese rounds with olive oil.

5 Bake the gougère in the oven until the dough is crusty and brown and the goats' cheese is toasted, 45–50 minutes. The gougère will puff, then deflate slightly as it cools. Serve it warm, cut in wedges.

Shortcut: Individual gougères, each topped with a round of goats' cheese, will take 10–15 minutes less to cook.

Getting Ahead: Gougère is best eaten at once, but it can be baked 2–3 hours ahead and reheated.

On the Side: In winter I'd favour a bowl of *Count Rocca's Minestrone* (page 52), and in summer a hearty salad of vegetables. You might like to try *Bulgarian Vegetable Salad* (page 83).

In the Glass: Gougère is Burgundian in origin, customary accompaniment to a chilled glass of kir (dry white wine with a teaspoon of cassis blackcurrant liqueur), or a fruity red Beaujolais.

Stromboli

Stromboli is a version of pizza where the dough is rolled with ham, pepperoni and cheese in a log, then sliced for serving. I've noticed that children are fascinated by yeast and the fact that it is alive and loves sugar, just like all of us. A family afternoon making bread dough for pizza will turn into a party, and even the smallest child can join in adding the topping. Here I'm suggesting a filling of meat and cheese, but the field is wide open for your own interpretation.

Serves 6

140 g/5 oz thinly sliced cooked ham
140 g/5 oz thinly sliced pepperoni sausage
75 g/2¹/₂ oz mozzarella cheese, shredded
75 g/2¹/₂ oz provolone cheese, shredded
2 tablespoons chopped herbs (parsley, basil, chives, etc.)
cornmeal or flour for baking sheets

For the pizza dough

7g/¹/₄ oz dry active yeast
125 ml/4 fl oz plus 2 tablespoons warm water
200 g/7 oz unbleached strong white flour, more for kneading
2 teaspoons sugar
¹/₂ teaspoon salt
2 tablespoons grated Parmesan cheese

1 For the pizza dough: sprinkle the yeast over 2 tablespoons warm water and leave until dissolved, about 5 minutes. Put the flour, sugar, salt and Parmesan cheese in a bowl and make a well in the centre. Mix the dissolved yeast with the remaining water and pour it into the well. Mix with your hands, gradually drawing in the flour to make a smooth dough. If it is sticky, add more flour a tablespoon at a time until the dough pulls from the sides of the bowl. Transfer the dough to a floured work surface and knead it until elastic and very smooth, 3–5 minutes. If you prefer, the dough can be mixed and kneaded in an electric mixer with the dough hook.

2 Oil a bowl, shape the dough into a ball and drop it into the bowl. Turn it so the top is oiled and cover the bowl with clingfilm. Leave it in a warm place until the dough is doubled in bulk, 1–1¹/₂ hours.

3 Knead the dough lightly to knock out air and roll it out on a floured work surface to a 25 x 35 cm/10 x 14 in rectangle. Cover the rectangle with ham slices, leaving a 2.5 cm/1 in border. Layer the pepperoni on top. Mix the cheeses and herbs in a bowl and sprinkle on top of the pepperoni. Starting at a long edge, roll the stromboli into a log and seal by pinching the side and ends. Place the log, seam-side down, on a baking sheet generously sprinkled with cornmeal or flour. Cover with a dry cloth and leave to rise until puffed, 15–20 minutes. Heat the oven to 230°C/450°F/Gas Mark 8, setting a heavy baking sheet on a low shelf.

4 Pull the baking sheet on the shelf halfway out of the oven. With a quick jerk, transfer the stromboli. Reduce the oven heat to 200°C/400°F/Gas Mark 6 and bake the stromboli until browned and a skewer inserted in the centre is hot to your touch when withdrawn, 30–40 minutes. Let the stromboli cool for 5–10 minutes before slicing with a serrated knife to serve. If you cut on the diagonal you'll have a longer and more impressive slice.

Shortcut: Use ready-made packaged or frozen pizza dough.

On the Side: A lively salad of chicory and rocket in a balsamic dressing.

In the Glass: Beer, wine, juice, milk, whatever is to your taste.

Pasta Pie with Peppery Greens

Kale, mustard greens, turnip greens and spring cabbage qualify for this pasta pie. To aerate and lighten it, I like to use shaped pasta such as spirals, bows or shells. For a vegetarian dish, leave out the sausagemeat and transform the pie into the Italian Easter speciality, torta pasquale, *by topping it after baking with halved hard-boiled eggs.*

1 Make the filling: wash the greens thoroughly, drain them in a colander and discard thick stems. Roll a few leaves loosely together and cut across into thin strips. Shred the rest of the greens in the same way. Heat the oil in a sauté pan or large shallow saucepan and crumble in the sausagemeat. Fry it, stirring constantly to break it up, until it is crumbly and brown, 4–6 minutes. Remove it with a draining spoon and set it aside.

2 Add the onions to the pan and fry them, stirring occasionally, until golden brown, 8–10 minutes. Stir in the garlic and allspice and cook for 1 minute. Stir in the shredded greens and pour over the chicken stock. Cook the greens, stirring occasionally, until wilted and just tender, 3–5 minutes. Stir in the sausagemeat, taste and adjust the seasoning. Leave the mixture to cool.

3 Heat the oven to 180°C/350°F/Gas Mark 4 and oil the baking dish. To cook the pasta: bring a large pan of salted water to the boil. Add the pasta and simmer it uncovered, stirring occasionally, until tender but still chewy (*al dente*), 8–12 minutes depending on the type of pasta. Drain it, rinse with hot water, and leave in the colander.

4 To assemble the pie: stir the eggs into the cooled filling of greens – it should be very moist. Spread about a third of the filling in the baking dish, top with some cannellini beans and cover with a third of the pasta. Sprinkle with Parmesan cheese. Add two more layers of greens, beans, pasta and cheese, ending with a layer of pasta and topping it generously with cheese.

5 Bake the pie in the oven until very hot and browned, 30–40 minutes.

Shortcut: Substitute two 280 g packages frozen chopped spinach for the kale.

Getting Ahead: Easy. Prepare up to two days ahead and keep in the refrigerator, or store it in the freezer for up to two months.

On the Side: A salad of sliced tomatoes for colour and fresh taste.

In the Glass: One of those light Italian reds that disappear so fast such as a Valpolicella or a Bardolino.

Serves 6

330 g/12 oz shaped pasta

1 large can (800 g) cooked cannellini beans, drained

125 g/4$\frac{1}{2}$ oz Parmesan cheese, grated

For the peppery greens filling

675 g/1$\frac{1}{2}$ lb kale or other peppery greens

2 tablespoons oil

225 g/8 oz spicy sausage, removed from casings

3 medium onions, chopped

2 garlic cloves, chopped

$\frac{1}{2}$ teaspoon ground allspice

500 ml/16 fl oz chicken stock

salt and pepper

2 eggs, beaten to mix

22 x 33 cm/9 x 13 in baking dish

Three-cheese Macaroni

Sooner or later, every expatriate has an overwhelming urge for the taste of home. For Janis McLean, American born and bred, it was six weeks in France before she finally succumbed and cooked that quintessentially American dish, macaroni and cheese, using her grandmother's recipe. 'It's one of my very first dishes, and still a bite fresh from my childhood!' she says. Janis uses three cheeses in her contemporary version, and penne or shell pasta can be substituted for the macaroni.

Serves 6 as a main dish

330 g/12 oz macaroni
90 g/3 oz soft goats' cheese
90 g/3 oz Roquefort or other blue cheese

For the cheddar cheese sauce
1 litre/1³/4 pints milk
90 g/3 oz butter, more for the baking dish
45 g/1¹/2 oz flour
1¹/4 teaspoons salt
1 teaspoon ground white pepper
170 g/6 oz mature Cheddar cheese, grated
2 teaspoons Dijon mustard

20 cm/8 in cast-iron skillet (or large
  baking dish)

1 Heat the oven to 190°C/375°F/Gas Mark 5. Bring a large pan of salted water to a rapid boil. Cook the pasta according to package directions until *al dente* – tender but still chewy. Drain the pasta in a colander and tip into a bowl.
2 Meanwhile, make the cheese sauce: scald the milk in a saucepan. Melt the butter in another saucepan, whisk in the flour and cook for 1–2 minutes. Do not let the flour brown. Take it from the heat, and whisk in the hot milk. Return the pan to the heat and bring the sauce to the boil, whisking constantly until it boils and thickens. Season with salt and pepper and simmer until the sauce generously coats the back of a spoon, 1–2 minutes. Add half the Cheddar cheese and stir until it is melted, ¹/2–1 minute. Take it at once from the heat as the cheese will form strings if it is overcooked. Whisk in the mustard, taste the sauce and adjust the seasoning. Be careful not to oversalt the sauce as the blue cheese will add more salt.
3 Stir the cheese sauce into the pasta and taste again for seasoning. Butter the skillet or baking dish – a cast-iron pan or gratin dish will give you a lovely crust. Spread half of the macaroni in the dish and crumble the goats' and blue cheese on top. Top with the remaining macaroni and spoon over any remaining sauce. Sprinkle the top with the reserved Cheddar cheese.
4 Bake the macaroni and cheese for 25–35 minutes until hot and bubbly. Turn on the grill for the last 5 minutes to brown the crust. Let the dish rest for 5–10 minutes before serving.

Getting Ahead: Macaroni cheese can be prepared 2–3 days ahead and kept in the refrigerator, or frozen for three months. To finish, thaw the dish if necessary and bake it in the oven as directed.

On the Side: Janis adds a little colour with sautéed cherry tomatoes and wilted spinach.

In the Glass: A robust red wine, nothing fancy but full-bodied enough to stand up to the cheese.

MADAME PARRET'S CHEESE TOASTS
(Serves 4)
Madame Parret is the wife of our cheese guru in Burgundy, a man who stocks more than 300 varieties of cheese in his cellars, aging them just like wine. Nothing goes to waste in a well run French kitchen, so it is not surprising that Madame has clever ideas for using leftover cheese. She likes to use Morbier, a creamy aged cheese that melts well, but other cheeses such as Gruyère, Brie, soft goats' cheese, even Cheddar, do equally well.

Heat the oven to 200°C/400°F/Gas Mark 6. Set 4 large slices of country bread, cut 1.25 cm/¹/2 in thick, in an oiled baking dish. Spoon 2 tablespoons wine over each slice. Thinly slice 225 g/8 oz cheese, including the rind, and arrange it on the bread to cover it completely. Sprinkle with a thinly sliced onion and salt and pepper. Bake in the oven until the cheese is melted and brown, 20–25 minutes. Serve very hot.

We're spoiled with potatoes nowadays. Even the average supermarket offers a half-dozen varieties, while farmers' markets overflow with potatoes in curious colours, shapes and sizes. Such oddities can be delicious, at their best simply boiled or steamed so their flavours – sweet, nutty or creamy – are best appreciated. The following recipes are more suited to a basic, everyday potato, preferably one of the floury types such as Maris Piper, designed for baking. These are the potatoes that cook to a crisp finish in hot fat, or fall agreeably into purée when thoroughly boiled. They take well to seasonings, too. Read on:

Laura's Accordion Potatoes

It was Canadian Laura Calder who showed me how to slice potatoes like hard-boiled eggs, but without quite cutting them apart, so they fan out in hot fat in the oven like an accordion. Any medium-sized potatoes will do and the choice of fat can include olive oil, butter mixed with vegetable oil, or best of all pan drippings from a roast. They're deliciously crispy, and I serve them with almost anything. (These are also known variously as Hasselback, Hedgehog or Toast-rack Potatoes.)

Heat the oven to 190°C/375°F/Gas Mark 5. Put each potato (unpeeled) in a tablespoon and cut them into vertical 6 mm/1/4 in slices – this neat trick with the spoon ensures they remain joined at the base. Open the potatoes slightly and insert 1–2 bay leaves or thyme sprigs in each one. Lay them in a baking dish just large enough to contain them. Sprinkle them with salt and pepper and pour a 1.25 cm/1/2 in layer of fat on top. Heat the potatoes on top of the stove until bubbling, then roast them in the oven, basting from time to time, until they are brown and crisp. Timing will vary from 3/4 to 1 hour, depending on their size.

Kate's Crispies (Serves 4)

Kate Rowe, editorial associate for this book, fried up these potatoes one day when a crowd of unexpected visitors arrived. They've been winners ever since.

Heat the oven to 220°C/425°F/Gas Mark 7. Peel 900 g/2 lb potatoes and cut them into 2.5 cm/1 in chunks. Toss them in a roasting pan with 175 ml/6 fl oz sunflower oil, 60 ml/2 fl oz olive oil, and a few sprigs of rosemary or thyme. Heat the potatoes on top of the stove for 3–5 minutes, until the oil is hot. Then roast them in the oven, stirring every 10–15 minutes, for 1–1 1/2 hours, until the potatoes are browned and very crisp. Don't worry if the potatoes stick to the pan at

the beginning – by the end of cooking, you will have delicious crispy bits. Season just before serving.

Spiced Spuds (Serves 6–8)

Potatoes roasted in the fat and juices beside a plump chicken or rib of beef are quite simply the best – try them with this sprinkling of spice, or leave them plain if you prefer.

Scrub 900 g/2 lb small new potatoes but do not peel them. Dry them on paper towels. In a large bowl, mix 1 teaspoon grated nutmeg, 1/2 teaspoon ground allspice, 1 teaspoon salt, 1/2 teaspoon pepper and 3–4 tablespoons drippings from a roast, or olive oil. Add the potatoes and toss until they are well coated. Spread the potatoes around a roast as it cooks, or put them in a separate roasting pan. Heat for 1 minute on top of the stove, then transfer them to an oven heated to 190°C/375°F/Gas Mark 5. Roast, stirring from time to time, until the potatoes are lightly browned and tender when pierced with a skewer, 35–45 minutes. If the oven temperature for a roast is hotter, the potatoes will cook more quickly, or if cooler, they will take longer. Either way, they will do fine.

Stovies (Serves 4)

Stovies, from the French *étuver*, to stew, are simmered with onions and stock until they are meltingly tender.

Heat 2 tablespoons vegetable oil with 1 tablespoon butter and fry 2 thinly sliced onions until golden brown, about 5 minutes. Then stir in 900 g/2 lb thinly sliced potatoes, sprinkle with salt and pepper, and spread them in a layer. Pour over about 500 ml/16 fl oz chicken or vegetable stock, enough to just cover the potatoes. Cover and simmer until the potatoes are tender, 15–20 minutes. Remove the lid and simmer until all the stock has evaporated, 10–15 minutes longer.

FLAVOURINGS FOR MASHED POTATOES

Roasted Garlic: Heat the oven to 180°C/350°F/Gas Mark 4. Allow a head of garlic per person and trim them so the tops of the cloves are exposed. Pack them in a small heavy pan and pour over enough olive oil to almost cover them. Cover tightly and roast them in the oven 1–1 1/2 hours, until the garlic is very tender. Drain them, reserving the oil, and add 3 tablespoons of the oil to the mashed potatoes instead of butter. Mash the garlic purée from the skins and stir it into the mashed potatoes. Taste and adjust the seasoning.

Goats' Cheese and Chives: Stir 110 g/4 oz fresh goats' cheese, cut into small pieces, and 3 tablespoons chopped chives into the finished mashed potatoes. Taste and adjust the seasoning.

I have been spending more time in California lately, because our daughter Emma lives in Los Angeles. The lifestyle there is famously different and so is the food. In the year-round warmth, the rich soups and leisurely, slowly cooked stews that suit a northern climate have no appeal. So I've picked up local habits and do much cooking outdoors on the barbecue. Even better are dishes that need no heat at all, hence the title of this chapter.

Many of the dishes I suggest here are salads, gathered from points as far apart as Bulgaria (cool and crunchy vegetables), and Australia (a zippy tartare of tuna with goats' cheese). Pear and fennel salad has a very Italian topping of Parmesan cheese, while my light version of *Waldorf Chicken Salad* is firmly native to the USA. Many of these salads can be prepared six hours or more ahead, so I think you'll be surprised by how practical they are. And you're bound to enjoy the two salads-in-a-sandwich that I've discovered, one from Provence, the other Middle Eastern in inspiration. Unlike most sandwiches, they hold up for several hours without refrigeration.

Many recipes that need no cooking rely on vigorous flavours such as garlic, chilli, anchovy or olive to make an instant impact. This principle is taken a step further in my collection of 'Cold Sauces and Dips', where you'll find versatile partners such as *Italian Green Sauce*, fragrant with herbs, salty with anchovy and excellent with fish. Many play multiple roles; for example *Hot Pepper Mayonnaise*, intended for fish soup, is delicious with crudités, and so on. My particular favourite is *Piquant Onion and Citrus Sauce* (*Escabeche*) from Spain, a lively mix of orange, lemon, vinegar, olive oil and lots of parsley. This is perfect with grilled vegetables.

I'm a lazy cook in warm weather. Aren't we all – there are far too many distractions to spend much time in the kitchen. So here's the last rule for no-cook suppers: the fewer the ingredients, the better. I also urge you to buy good-quality main ingredients already cooked – ham, chicken and prawns are examples you can rely on – then add your own personal dressing. If there's a bottled dressing that you really like, by all means use it, though I have to say I have not yet found one with which I am really happy.

No-cook Suppers and Salads

Pear and Fennel Salad with Parmesan

For best effect, arrange alternating slices of pears and fennel in a fan shape on the plate, then add shavings of Parmesan cheese. To this very Italian combination, I like to add some pine nuts. You may be able to find them ready-toasted, but if not they are much improved if you have a chance to brown them in a dry, non-stick frying pan on top of the stove for 2–3 minutes. Take care as they scorch easily. This salad can act as appetizer, dessert or even a light main course if you add a bit more cheese.

1 Trim the root and top of the fennel bulb and discard any tough outer leaves. Halve it and slice each half very thinly, if possible on the mandoline. Peel and halve the pears. Scoop out the cores and stem ends, using a melon baller or small spoon. Cut each half into thin crescent slices. Brush them with lemon juice so they do not discolour and cover tightly with clingfilm, pressing it down so all air is excluded.
2 For the dressing: whisk the balsamic vinegar, mustard, salt and pepper in a small bowl until mixed. Gradually whisk in the oil so the dressing emulsifies and thickens slightly. Taste and adjust the seasoning.
3 Shortly before serving: wash and dry the watercress, discard the stems, and arrange the sprigs on four individual plates. Arrange the pear and fennel slices on top. Whisk the dressing lightly to re-emulsify it, then spoon it over the pears and fennel. Sprinkle with pine nuts and shave a few slices of Parmesan on to each plate. Serve the salad as soon as possible, within a half-hour.

Shortcut: Simplify the salad presentation: peel and halve the pears without slicing them. Toss the sliced fennel with vinaigrette and arrange it on serving plates, with a pear half on the side. Spoon over the remaining dressing, and sprinkle with pine nuts and cheese.

Getting Ahead: The fennel and pear can be sliced, and the dressing made up to 2 hours ahead. Keep everything at room temperature. Wash the watercress and assemble the salad just before serving.

On the Side: Focaccia, from your favourite bakery.

In the Glass: A glass of Marsala would make a marriage from heaven.

Serves 4

1 medium fennel bulb (about 225 g/8 oz)
2 medium ripe pears
juice of 1 lemon
1 bunch watercress (about 90 g/3 oz)
40 g/1^1/$_2$ oz pine nuts
60 g/2 oz piece of Parmesan cheese (for shaving)

For the dressing
3 tablespoons balsamic vinegar
^{1}/$_2$ teaspoon Dijon mustard
salt and pepper
125 ml/4 fl oz olive oil

Smoked Trout Mousse with Celery Salsa

This mousse is deliciously rich, so I like to serve it with a contrasting crispy salsa made with celery. If you can't find green peppercorns, flavour it with fresh or bottled grated horseradish. Instead of trout you can substitute the same weight of smoked salmon.

Serves 6 as a light main course

vegetable oil, for the ramekins

4–6 smoked trout fillets (about 330 g/12 oz total)

140 g/5 oz walnut halves

2 tablespoons green peppercorns in brine or vinegar, rinsed and drained

280 g/10 oz soft cheese, such as Philadelphia

300 ml/10 fl oz double cream, more if needed

juice of 1 lemon, or to taste

For the salsa

4 celery sticks

medium bunch of watercress (about 90 g/3 oz)

2 tablespoons walnut oil

2 tablespoons red wine or cider vinegar

salt and pepper

6 ramekins (175 ml/6 fl oz capacity each)

1 Brush the ramekins with oil, then line each base with a round of non-stick baking paper. Flake the trout with a fork or your fingers, discarding the skin and any bones. Set aside six walnut halves for decoration and coarsely chop the rest. Chop the green peppercorns.

2 Beat the cheese to soften it, then beat in the cream until the cheese just falls from a spoon – the amount of cream depends very much on the stiffness of the cheese. If needed, thin the mixture with extra cream or a couple of spoonfuls of milk. Stir in the chopped green peppercorns and lemon juice, followed by the trout and chopped walnuts. Taste and adjust the seasoning – as the trout may be salty and the green peppercorns strong, you may not need much more salt and pepper. Pack the mousse mixture into the ramekins, smooth the surface and press a piece of baking paper on top. Chill until firm, at least 2 hours.

3 Make the salsa: slice each piece of celery lengthwise in 3–4 thin sticks, then cut crosswise into dice. Strip the watercress leaves from the stems, set aside a handful of the leaves and coarsely shred the remainder. Stir the shredded leaves into the celery with the oil, vinegar, salt and pepper. Taste, adjust the seasoning and chill.

4 To finish, place the reserved watercress leaves on each serving plate. Discard the paper from each mousse, then run a knife around the sides of each one and turn them out on to the watercress. Remove the lining paper and top each mousse with a spoonful of the salsa and a walnut half.

Getting Ahead: Make the mousse up to two days ahead, store it in the refrigerator and turn it out just before serving. The salsa can be made only 2 hours ahead as the watercress wilts rapidly.

On the Side: Scandinavian-style crispbread provides a contrast to the creamy mousse.

In the Glass: Following the Scandinavian theme, let's go for a tot of ice-cold aquavit or Russian vodka.

Tuna and Goats' Cheese Tartare

This east–west version of tuna tartare is inspired by the famed Tetsuya Wakuda, the Australian chef, who combines Asian and Western flavours to brilliant effect. Tuna tartare should be served very cold and as soon as the seasonings have been added, so the fish retains its sea freshness.

Serves 4 as an appetizer

450 g/1 lb piece of tuna, well chilled

60 g/2 oz fresh goats' cheese, chopped

3 shallots, very finely chopped

For the dressing

3 tablespoons rice wine vinegar or lemon juice

2 teaspoons soy sauce, more to taste

1 teaspoon *nam pla* (Thai fish sauce), or 1 fillet of anchovy, finely chopped

2 tablespoons capers, drained and chopped

2.5 cm/1 in piece of fresh root ginger, chopped

pinch of cayenne pepper

2–3 tablespoons olive oil

2 tablespoons snipped chives

1 It is important to chill the tuna thoroughly and then to handle it as lightly as possible using a very sharp knife. Trim the fish, removing all skin and membrane. Slice it in strips, and finally crosswise into 6 mm/$1/4$ in dice. Put it in a chilled bowl and stir in the goats' cheese and shallots.

2 Make the dressing: in a separate bowl whisk together the rice wine vinegar or lemon juice, soy sauce, *nam pla* or anchovy, capers, ginger and cayenne. Gradually whisk in the olive oil so the dressing emulsifies and thickens slightly.

3 Just before serving: stir the dressing into the tuna with half of the chives, tossing as gently as possible with two forks. Taste and adjust the seasoning of the tartare with any of the flavourings. Pile the tartare on chilled plates, sprinkle with the remaining chives and serve it well chilled, as soon as possible.

Getting Ahead: You can chop the tuna, chill it and make the dressing up to 2 hours ahead. Toss them together only just before serving.

On the Side: I like to serve cups of iceberg lettuce for guests to use as wrappers for the tartare. However if finger food is a problem, shred the lettuce and mound the tartare on top.

In the Glass: Some chilled sake rice wine would be perfect for me, but a chilled white Muscadet or Sauvignon Blanc is a possibility, too.

Avocado, Grapefruit and Prawn Salad with a Citrus Dressing

The pink of prawns and grapefruit with the green of avocado and rocket make a cheerful welcome in hot weather. Personally, I prefer the meltingly rich Hass avocados that have a charcoal skin, but smooth green juicier avocados have their devotees too.

1 To remove sections from the grapefruits: slice off the top and base of the fruits. Following the curve of the fruit, cut away the skin, zest and pith so only the segments and central membranes are left. Slide the knife down each side of a section to cut it free of the membranes, letting the section fall into the bowl. Continue cutting, turning the membranes back like the pages of a book, until you've removed all of the sections. Chill them and reserve the juice.

2 Wash and dry the rocket. Halve each avocado lengthwise, cutting down to the stone. Twist the halves and pull them from the stone. Tap the blade of a knife sharply on to the stone, twist and pull out the stone. Peel away the skin and cut the avocado flesh into lengthwise slices. Brush some of the grapefruit juice over the slices so they do not discolour.

3 For the dressing: whisk the reserved grapefruit juice with the lemon juice, onion, garlic, mustard, salt and pepper until mixed. Gradually add the olive oil, whisking constantly so the dressing emulsifies and thickens slightly. Taste, adjust the seasoning and set aside.

4 Shortly before serving: toss the rocket with about a third of the dressing and taste for seasoning. Spread a bed of rocket on four plates. Arrange the avocado slices and grapefruit sections like the spokes of a wheel on top and spoon over more dressing. Chop the dill and toss with the prawns and remaining dressing. Taste, adjust the seasoning and spoon the prawns into the centre of the wheel. Serve the salad as soon as you can so the greens do not wilt.

Shortcut: Substitute a can of grapefruit segments for the fresh fruit and you may be surprised at the happy results.

Getting Ahead: The grapefruits, rocket and avocado can be prepared up to 4 hours ahead and kept, tightly covered, in the refrigerator. Keep the dressing at room temperature. Assemble the salad just before you serve it.

On the Side: Some crisp toasts or freshly baked bread such as the *Anadama* or *Cracked Wheat Bread* (page 49).

In the Glass: We've a lot going on here – tart grapefruit, rich avocado, peppery rocket. I'd suggest a mild, pleasant white Muscadet, or a rosé from Anjou just to the east.

Serves 4 as a main course

3 large pink grapefruits
110 g/4 oz rocket
2 avocados
225 g/8 oz cooked peeled prawns
3–4 dill sprigs

For the dressing
juice of 1/2 lemon
1/2 sweet red onion, finely chopped
1 garlic clove, chopped
1 teaspoon Dijon mustard
salt and pepper
125 ml/4 fl oz olive oil

Chicken Salad with Cherries and Rocket

The delights of duck with cherries are well known, but cherries are also delicious with chicken as a summer salad. For a party dish, replace the chicken with skinless duck breasts cooked the same way.

1 Cut the chicken breasts into 2.5 cm/1 in cubes. Stone the cherries and mix them in a bowl with the chicken. Trim and slice the spring onions, including some of the green tops, and add to the chicken. For decoration, cut the remaining tops into thin strips and soak them in iced water so that they curl. Wash and dry the rocket. If the leaves are large, tear them in two or three pieces.
2 Make the dressing: whisk the lemon juice, mustard, ginger, ground coriander, salt and pepper in a small bowl until mixed. Gradually whisk in the olive oil so the dressing emulsifies and thickens slightly. Taste and adjust the seasoning.
3 Toss the rocket in about a quarter of the dressing, taste the greens for seasoning and arrange them on four plates. Toss the chicken and cherries with the coriander and remaining dressing. Taste and adjust the seasoning. Pile the salad on the greens and sprinkle with sesame seeds. Drain the spring onion strips and scatter them on top.

Serves 4 for supper

4 cooked boneless, skinless chicken
  breasts (about 550 g/1¼ lb total)
225 g/8 oz cherries
4 spring onions
225 g/8 oz rocket or other tart greens
1½ tablespoons sesame seeds, toasted

For the dressing

juice of 2 lemons
1 teaspoon Dijon mustard
2.5 cm/1 in piece of fresh root ginger,
  finely chopped
1 teaspoon ground coriander
salt and pepper
125 ml/4 fl oz olive oil
2 tablespoons chopped coriander

Shortcut: Don't bother to stone the cherries, but be sure to warn your guests!

Getting Ahead: Cut up the chicken, stone the cherries, prepare the greens and make the dressing up to 6 hours ahead, keeping chicken, cherries and greens in the refrigerator. Assemble the salad just before serving.

On the Side: Bread. Crisp baguette or a flat pitta are perfect, whatever is your pleasure.

In the Glass: A well chilled white or rosé with some acidity to contrast with the sweet cherries.

TO STONE CHERRIES

You can stone cherries two ways: the quickest is to use a cherry stoning tool which operates like scissors and pops out the stone like a bullet, leaving a somewhat mangled cherry. Slower but less destructive is to scoop out the stone with the point of a vegetable peeler, leaving the cherry more or less intact. Less orthodox but efficient implements include hairpins, large hair grips and paper clips.

Waldorf Chicken Salad

I've lightened this winter classic by substituting yoghurt for some of the mayonnaise that traditionally binds and adds richness to the salad. A crisp, tart apple is best, such as Gala, Fuji or Braeburn, and I always leave on the skins for colour.

Serves 6 as an appetizer, 4 as a main course

125 g/4^1/$_2$ oz walnut pieces

4 cooked boneless, skinless chicken breasts
  (about 550 g/1^1/$_4$ lb total)

4 celery sticks

450 g/1 lb tart, crisp apples

1 lemon

175 ml/6 fl oz natural yoghurt

175 ml/6 fl oz mayonnaise

salt and pepper

1 Toast the walnut pieces (page 166). With your fingers, pull the chicken breasts into slivers about 5 cm/2 in long. Peel the strings from the celery sticks with a vegetable peeler and slice them crosswise at an angle in 6 mm/^{1}/$_4$ in slices. I also like to reserve the celery tops for decoration as their pretty green fronds tell what you'll find in the salad.

2 Halve and core the apples, and then dice them. Transfer them to a large bowl.

3 Cut the lemon in half, squeeze the juice over the diced apples and toss to coat them so they do not discolour. Add the chicken, celery, yoghurt, mayonnaise and two-thirds of the walnut pieces. Season with salt and pepper. Stir the ingredients together until combined, taste and adjust the seasoning. Cover, and chill the salad for at least an hour.

4 To finish: coarsely chop the remaining walnut pieces. Pile the salad into individual bowls, or one large bowl. Sprinkle with chopped walnuts and decorate with celery leaves.

Getting Ahead: Waldorf salad keeps well for up to 24 hours in the refrigerator. Just before serving, stir it and add a squeeze of lemon juice if the flavour seems flat.

On the Side: Something with cheese – ready-made cheese straws would be perfect.

In the Glass: A light red wine such as a Beaujolais (Gamay).

POACHED CHICKEN BREASTS

It is fine to buy cooked chicken breasts for these two salads, but if you poach them yourself the meat will be more moist and succulent. Let the breasts cool in the liquid, and then drain and pull them into slivers about 5 cm/2 in long – they will taste less dry than if cut with a knife.

In a shallow saucepan, combine 575 ml/1 pint water with 1 small onion, sliced, a 2.5 cm/1 in piece of fresh root ginger, sliced, 1 tablespoon soy sauce, 2 teaspoons crushed coriander seeds, and the pared zest of 1 lemon. Cover, bring to the boil and simmer for 10 minutes. Strip out the sinew on the underside of each chicken breast. Let the broth cool for 1–2 minutes, then add the chicken breasts, pushing them down so they are submerged. Cover, bring to the boil and simmer for 2 minutes. Leave them, still covered, until cool before draining them. If keeping the breasts longer than half an hour, store them in the refrigerator, in the liquid.

Winter Salad of Country Ham with Beetroot, Chicory and Lamb's Lettuce

Chicory and lamb's lettuce are among the treats of winter, a glimpse of green among the seasonal roots on the vegetable stall. Teamed with beetroot for colour and hazelnuts for crunch, they are a classic French combination, delicious with thinly sliced smoked dry-cured ham, or some imported prosciutto.

Serves 4 for supper

75 g/2¹/₂ oz hazelnuts
450 g/1 lb cooked baby beetroot
2 heads (about 225 g/8 oz) chicory
170 g/6 oz lamb's lettuce
330 g/12 oz thinly sliced ham

For the dressing
2 tablespoons red wine vinegar
salt and pepper
1 teaspoon Dijon mustard
75 ml/2¹/₂ fl oz walnut oil

1 Toast and peel the hazelnuts (page 166). Trim the beetroots and slip off the skins with your fingers. Cut the beetroots in quarters or leave them whole depending on size. Trim the chicory, discarding any browned outer leaves. Cut the heads diagonally into 6 mm/¹/₄ in slices.

2 Trim the roots of the lamb's lettuce and discard any wilted leaves, leaving them in bunches. Soak them in a sink of water for 15 minutes, shaking to loosen grit between the leaves – even the cleanest lamb's lettuce seems to trap earth in the crevices. Lift out the bunches, rinsing each one under running water to remove grit, and drain thoroughly. Combine the lamb's lettuce and chicory in a bowl.

3 For the dressing: whisk the vinegar, salt, pepper and mustard in a bowl. Gradually whisk in the oil so the dressing emulsifies and thickens slightly. Taste it, adjust the seasoning and pour about half over the greens. Toss them and taste again for seasoning.

4 Pile the greens on four plates and sprinkle with the hazelnuts. Curl the ham slices and arrange them on top with beetroot round the edge. Spoon the remaining dressing over the beetroot and serve the salad within 15 minutes so the greens do not wilt.

Shortcut: You'll gain a bit of time by buying hazelnuts already peeled.

Getting Ahead: Make the dressing and prepare all the ingredients ready to go and store them in the refrigerator for up to 8 hours. Dress the greens and assemble the salad just before serving.

On the Side: A hearty slice of country bread.

In the Glass: Red wine, robust and warming. Go for a Shiraz or a Zinfandel.

Cherry Tomato Salad with Wholegrain Mustard and Tarragon

Flavours blend wonderfully well in this simple little salad. Walnut oil adds a touch of luxury but olive oil can be used instead. To make this a more substantial course, add some cold roast chicken.

Serves 4–6 as an appetizer

900 g/2 lb cherry tomatoes
60 g/2 oz walnut pieces

For the mustard-tarragon dressing
small bunch of tarragon (about 30 g/1 oz)
2 tablespoons balsamic vinegar
1¹/₂ tablespoons wholegrain Dijon mustard
salt and pepper
125 ml/4 fl oz walnut oil or olive oil

1 Peel the tomatoes (page 166). Peeling them may seem tiresome, but in this case it is well worth doing, so the tomato juice runs and mixes with the dressing.
2 Make the dressing: strip the tarragon leaves from their stems, setting some sprigs aside for decoration. Coarsely chop the leaves. Whisk the vinegar with the mustard, salt and pepper in a small bowl. Gradually whisk in the oil so that the dressing emulsifies and thickens slightly. Whisk in the chopped tarragon, taste and adjust the seasoning.
3 Put the tomatoes into a salad bowl. Pour the dressing over the tomatoes, mixing carefully, and taste again for seasoning. Shortly before serving, sprinkle the tomatoes with walnuts and top with tarragon sprigs.

Getting Ahead: *Cherry Tomato Salad* can be made and kept at room temperature for 2–3 hours, and the flavours will mellow in that time.

On the Side: Plenty of crusty bread to absorb the dressing.

In the Glass: Here's the place for one of those colourful Mediterranean apéritifs such as Campari, Lillet, Dubonnet, or a red or white vermouth.

Bulgarian Vegetable Salad

This refreshing salad of diced vegetables, including cucumber, tomato and red pepper, is the universal Bulgarian appertizer known as shopska. *Flavours are intense, textures an intriguing balance of juicy, chewy and crisp. Locally,* shopska *always comes as a first course, served with a glass of mastika, a white brandy. However, I find it a satisfying lunch salad, too, when it is topped with hard-boiled eggs and a grating of feta cheese.*

1 Mix the onion in a large bowl with the vinegar, lemon juice, salt and pepper and leave to soften for 10–15 minutes. Peel the cucumber, cut it lengthwise in half and scoop out the seeds with a teaspoon. Cut each half lengthwise into 3–4 strips, then crosswise into dice. Cut the pepper in half, discard the core, seeds and ribs, and finely dice the flesh. Seed and dice the tomatoes (page 166) but don't bother to peel them.

2 Put the vegetables with the onion and stir until mixed. Stir in the olive oil with more lemon juice, salt and pepper to your taste. Cover and leave to marinate at room temperature for 1–2 hours.

3 To finish: chop half of the parsley, stir it into the salad, taste, and adjust the seasoning again. Mound the salad on serving plates, flatten it slightly and sprinkle it with grated cheese. Surround the salad with quarters of hard-boiled egg, olives and remaining sprigs of parsley.

Getting Ahead: Prepare up to 5 hours ahead and keep it in the refrigerator. Let it return to room temperature, then arrange it on plates just before serving.

On the Side: Serve pitta or another flat bread. It may encourage your guests to treat the salad as finger food, but that's all to the good.

In the Glass: For a Balkan touch, serve a glass of anise-flavoured ouzo or arak.

Serves 6 as appetizer, 4 as a main course

1 onion, diced
2 tablespoons wine vinegar
2 teaspoons lemon juice, more to taste
salt and pepper
1 large cucumber
1 large red pepper
3 medium tomatoes
75 ml/2^1/$_2$ fl oz olive oil

For garnish
bunch of flatleaf parsley (about 40 g/1^1/$_2$ oz)
60 g/2 oz grated cheese
4 hard-boiled eggs, quartered
90 g/3 oz black olives

Provençal Tomato Sandwich

Provençal Tomato Sandwich, *or* Pan Bagnat, *comes from around Nice, where it is
known as* pain baigné, *meaning 'bathed bread'. I often think of it as salad Niçoise in
a sandwich and, like salad Niçoise, it can include all sorts of ingredients, such as hard-
boiled eggs, gherkins, sliced sweet onion or shallot with the mandatory tomato, tuna,
olives, garlic, capers, and anchovy. Everything is layered in a baguette or a roll, then
drizzled with an olive oil vinaigrette, wrapped and pressed so the tomato juices and
flavourings meld in one glorious salad. Hot weather food at its finest!*

Serves 4

1 baguette

2 hard-boiled eggs, sliced

1 x 170 g can tuna in water, drained
and flaked

3–4 anchovy fillets, chopped

1 shallot, chopped

90 g/3 oz stoned black or green olives,
chopped

1 tablespoon capers, rinsed, drained
and chopped

2 large tomatoes (about 330 g/12 oz),
cored and sliced

2–3 gherkins, thinly sliced (optional)

For the vinaigrette dressing

3 tablespoons red wine vinegar

1 teaspoon Dijon mustard

1 garlic clove, very finely chopped

salt and pepper

125 ml/4 fl oz extra virgin olive oil

1 Make the vinaigrette dressing: whisk the vinegar with the mustard, garlic, salt
and pepper until mixed. Gradually whisk in the oil, starting drop by drop,
then pouring in a slow stream, whisking constantly so that the dressing
emulsifies and thickens slightly. Slit the baguette lengthwise pulling out some
of the crumb with your fingers. Brush the insides of the baguette generously
with vinaigrette dressing.

2 To fill the sandwich: line up the sliced eggs in the bottom of the baguette and
top with flaked tuna. Sprinkle with some of the anchovy, shallot, olives and
capers, and spoon over some dressing. Top with tomato, overlapping the
slices, add the gherkins if using and sprinkle with the remaining anchovy,
shallot, olives and capers. Moisten with more dressing. It's at this stage that I
assess the situation. Perhaps all the dressing is not needed as the tomatoes are
extra juicy. Do they need a sprinkling of salt and pepper? How about some
herbs? – I would say yes, but they are not traditional. So do what you like
and make the sandwich your own.

3 Add the upper half of the baguette and press it down well. Wrap tightly in
clingfilm and weight the baguette down so the tomato juices permeate and
soften the bread. Bricks are a bit much, but a couple of roasting pans with a
heavy saucepan in each can be just right. Leave for 1–2 hours at room temperature. Unwrap the *Pan Bagnat* when you're ready to eat, and slice it for
serving.

Getting Ahead: It is essential to make *Pan Bagnat* at least an hour ahead so flavours
mellow and the bread soaks up the tomato juices. It keeps well for up to 4 hours, and
no chilling is necessary – perfect picnic fare.

On the Side: Some goats' cheese, that does well in the sun, with seasonal fruits for
dessert.

In the Glass: A chilled Provençal rosé.

Lavash Wrap

Lavash is a staple bread of the Middle East, used either for dipping or wrapping, and good to have on hand. The soft, pliable ovals measure about 25 x 10 cm/10 x 4 in, a hearty single serving, so here I'm allowing one for two people. I'm suggesting just one combination for a wrapped sandwich, but the possibilities are many.

Serves 4

1 avocado

1 lemon, halved

1 medium cucumber

2 lavash breads

125 ml/4 fl oz Turkish Tarator Sauce
  (see below)

4 thin slices of cooked turkey (about
  170 g/6 oz)

110 g/4 oz bitter greens such as rocket

60 g/2 oz feta cheese, crumbled

90 g/3 oz stoned black olives

TURKISH TARATOR SAUCE

(Makes 375 ml/12 fl oz, to serve 6)

Tarator can be made with walnuts or hazelnuts and is a versatile accompaniment to boiled vegetables, cold chicken or seafood. On its own with pitta bread, it's almost a meal in itself. Tarator keeps well, so any left-over from the lavash will not be wasted.

  Discard crusts from 2 slices of white bread, and soak them in water for 10 minutes. Squeeze dry and put in a processor with 100 g/3 1/2 oz walnut pieces or toasted hazelnuts (page 166), 2–3 crushed and peeled garlic cloves, salt and pepper. Work until just puréed. Add 60 ml/2 fl oz wine vinegar and work for 1–2 seconds. With the blades turning, gradually beat in 150 ml/5 fl oz olive oil. Taste and adjust the seasoning. The sauce can be stored in the refrigerator for up to a week; pour a thin layer of olive oil on top to prevent it from drying out. Let it come to room temperature before serving.

1 Halve the avocado lengthwise, twist the halves apart and discard the stone. Peel the halves, cut them in crescents and sprinkle with lemon juice so they do not discolour. Peel the cucumber, cut it in half lengthwise and scoop out the seeds with a teaspoon. Cut the halves lengthwise in strips, then crosswise in 5 cm/2 in sticks – cutting sticks instead of slices holds the sandwich together.

2 Spread the lavash with the tarator sauce, leaving a 1.25 cm/^{1}/$_2$ in border all around. Layer the turkey, avocado, cucumber, and two-thirds of the greens on top and sprinkle with the cheese and olives. Reserve the remaining greens for garnish. Roll up each lavash quite tightly, starting at one of the long edges.

3 Cut the cylinders in four sections, lining them up so they are equal in length. Set two sections on each of four serving plates and decorate with the reserved greens.

Shortcut: You'll save some time by substituting ready-made hummus or tapenade for the tarator sauce.

Getting Ahead: Wrap in clingfilm and refrigerate them up to 4 hours. They will keep fine for 2 hours longer without being chilled.

On the Side: More greens, or perhaps some cherry tomatoes.

In the Glass: A light red wine.

Chefs are terrific at brightening dishes that seem depressed. A vivid sprinkling of fresh herbs, a topping of toasted cheese, a crispy pastry garnish can work wonders. Best of all is a lively little sauce on the side, something punchy to pick up the taste as well as the appearance. When freshly made, the flavours are all the more potent.

Piquant Onion and Citrus Sauce (*Escabeche*)

(Makes 375 ml/12 fl oz, serves 4–6)

Pour this sauce over hot or cold baked fish and leave to marinate in the refrigerator at least 12 hours. It is also good with roasted vegetables.

Combine 1 small onion, cut in pieces, 1 garlic clove, the pared zest of 1 orange and pared zest of 1 lemon, sprigs from a medium bunch of parsley, 2 teaspoons paprika, pinch of cayenne, 125 ml/4 fl oz olive oil, 3 tablespoons red wine vinegar, salt and pepper in a food processor or blender and work them to a purée. Taste and adjust the seasoning. The sauce keeps well in the refrigerator up to three days.

Scandinavian Dill-mustard Sauce

(Makes 375 ml/12 fl oz, serves 6)

This traditional sauce for gravlax and other marinated fish is good with baked ham, too.

In a small bowl, whisk together 2 tablespoons brown sugar, 3 tablespoons vinegar, 60 ml/2 fl oz mustard, 2 egg yolks, salt and pepper. Slowly add 250 ml/8 fl oz vegetable oil, whisking constantly until the mixture begins to thicken and emulsify. Add the oil in a steady stream, continuing to whisk vigorously. Stir in 3 table-spoons chopped dill and taste for seasoning. The sauce should taste of mustard without being overpowering. Store it in the refrigerator for not more than a day.

Asian Hot Chilli Dip

(Makes 250 ml/8 fl oz, serves 4– 6)

Good for all barbecued meats and poultry.

Halve and core 2 small jalapeño chillies, then finely chop them including the seeds. (Be careful not to touch your face or eyes after handling the chillies.) Heat 2 tablespoons vegetable oil in a small saucepan, add the chillies and 2 chopped garlic cloves and fry just until fragrant, about 1 minute. Take from the heat and stir in 75 ml/2¹/₂ fl oz soy sauce, 3 tablespoons rice wine vinegar, the juice of 1 lime and 3 tablespoons chopped coriander. Let the dip cool. It can be kept for two days in the refrigerator.

Italian Green Sauce (*Salsa Verde*)

(Makes 375 ml/12 fl oz, serves 3–4)

Try this variation of familiar pesto with pasta, fried fish or roast lamb. When freshly made, the sauce is fragrant with herbs; when stored the flavour mellows.

Discard the crusts from 2 slices of white bread and soak them in a small bowl, with enough red wine vinegar to cover, for 10 minutes. Squeeze the bread dry and put it in a food processor. Add the sprigs from 1 large bunch of parsley, 3 tablespoons capers, drained and rinsed, 4 crushed and peeled garlic cloves and 4 anchovy fillets and work to a purée. With the motor running, gradually add 150 ml/5 fl oz olive oil. Taste and adjust the seasoning. *Green Sauce* can be kept covered in the refrigerator for up to two days. It will separate slightly on standing and should be stirred before you serve it at room temperature

Hot Pepper Mayonnaise (*Sauce Rouille*)

(Makes 300 ml/10 fl oz, serves 4–6)

Rouille means rust, the colour of this sauce; if it looks pale don't hesitate to add a teaspoon of tomato purée. Serve with fish soups and stews, and hard-boiled eggs.

Remove the seeds of a fresh chilli and chop it, or soak a dried chilli in boiling water for 30 minutes, drain and then chop it. Soak 1 slice of white bread, crust removed, in water and squeeze it dry. Work the chilli, bread, 4 cloves of crushed and peeled garlic, 1 egg yolk, salt and pepper in a small food processor. With the motor running, gradually add 175 ml/6 fl oz olive oil, a teaspoonful at a time. When it starts to thicken and emulsify, the rest of the oil can be poured in a thin, steady stream. Taste and adjust the seasoning. *Hot Pepper Mayonnaise* can be mild or quite piquant, to your taste, so add a pinch of cayenne pepper if you like it hot. It should not be kept more than a day, even in the refrigerator, as it contains raw egg yolk. The egg yolk can be omitted, and then the mayonnaise can be made up to three days ahead.

TIPS FOR DIPS

Pitta Chips Heat the oven to 180°C/350°F/Gas Mark 4. Slit open two rounds of pitta bread and pull apart the two layers. Brush the rough, interior side with 60 ml/2 fl oz olive oil that has been heated for a minute with a teaspoon of ground cumin and a tea-spoon of ground coriander. Cut the bread in triangles and bake in the oven until very lightly browned and crisp, 6–8 minutes. The chips can be stored in an airtight container for a day or two.

Baked or Fried Tortilla Chips So much more tasty than the commercial kind! Serve tortilla chips on their own to nibble, or as nachos with a topping or dip of salsa or guacamole. Cut thin corn or flour tortillas into six wedges. To fry them: heat deep fat to 190°C/375°F and fry the chips until crisp and lightly browned, 1/2–1 minute. Drain them thoroughly. To bake chips: heat the oven to 190°C/375°F/Gas Mark 5. Brush the wedges with olive oil, sprinkle with coarse salt and bake until very crisp, 10–12 minutes. Whole tortillas, baked this way as a single round, are called *tostadas* and form the delicious crisp base for Mexican-style toppings. Store chips in an airtight container up to a week.

A day without wine is a day without sunshine they say, and for me that's also true of vegetables. This cheerful chapter looks at how I personally like to cook them. The title, 'lightly vegetarian', works in two ways. The recipes are light in themselves, though almost all of them can stand alone as main courses as well as accompany more substantial dishes. And I lightly take liberties with vegetarian rules, as I often cook vegetables with cheese, bacon, butter and even lard, the forgotten animal fat (tofu is not part of my vocabulary).

At home we have a salad at least once a day, and any meat or fish is surrounded by a bevy of cooked vegetables, fresh from the garden if the season is right. In spring it's baby carrots, peas, spinach, with a wealth of tomatoes and green beans in summer. Peppers and aubergine demand too much water for our chalky soil, but we make up for them with half a dozen kinds of squash. Old Monsieur Milbert, turning 82, masterminds all this single-handedly and he's been at it nearly 70 years. His speciality is roots, dominated by the onion family including shallots, garlic, chives, onion chives and tree onions (just for fun). His leeks last nine months of the year, from autumn and on to winter and the warmth of April. Floury potatoes, crisp root celery, beetroot and turnip are routine, while we chomp on what surely must be the world's best Brussels sprouts.

Aren't you envious? All this is to urge you to buy seasonally from an artisan producer. Vegetables, together with fruit, benefit more than any ingredient when they are locally grown on a small scale. They need little help in the kitchen – a sprinkling of cheese or a topping of cream sauce is often enough. Crisp pastry, such as the topping on *Wild Mushroom Pie*, adds a further dimension. I'm a great proponent of vegetable gratins, with their herbal flavourings and appetizing brown toppings. There's a happy trio of gratins in this chapter, one each for spring, summer and winter. As a way to present vegetables, enhanced but not hidden by their golden brown crust, a gratin seems to me ideal. Even when dressed in a white sauce, the colour and shapes of the vegetables still show through, and nuts, chopped herbs and other flavourings only add to the riot of colour. The special shallow dishes about 5 cm/2 in deep designed for gratins are such fun too; they come in all sorts of shapes, colours and sizes, often with little eared handles so they are easy to take from the oven. I must have a couple of dozen of them – I'm a gratin-dish junkie.

Tomato sauce in its many variations plays a double role in vegetarian cooking, either as accompaniment to another vegetable as in *Mexican Stuffed Peppers with Cheese*, or with a starch, particularly pasta. In this chapter you'll find a handful of different pasta sauces, all based on tomato. As for rice, red wine is the theme of my favourite risotto; it can easily be supplemented with a variety of vegetables, or with fish if you're feeling so inclined.

Lightly Vegetarian

Gratin of Summer Vegetables in Mint Pesto

At home we make this recipe all summer long with vegetables from the market. Then, in early September, the magic moment arrives when every ingredient comes from our own garden. The name 'pesto' comes from the Italian pestare, to pound, *as with a mortar and pestle. Basil is the traditional choice of aromatic herb but others, such as flatleaf parsley or coriander, are just as good. Mint is my particular favourite – an underestimated herb, I think.*

1 Heat the oven to 180°C/350°F/Gas Mark 4. Wipe the courgettes and squash with damp paper towels and cut them roughly into 2 cm/³/4 in chunks. Toss them into a large bowl. Cut the tomatoes in chunks, discarding the cores, and add them to the courgette and squash with the onions, salt and pepper. Brush the gratin dish with olive oil.

2 Make the pesto: tear the mint leaves from the stems, discarding the stems, and, if you like, reserve some sprigs for decoration. Purée the mint leaves, garlic, cheese and pine nuts in the food processor with 2–3 tablespoons of the olive oil. Gradually add the remaining oil with the blades turning so that the sauce emulsifies. It should be a rather loose consistency, thinner than mayonnaise but thicker than salad dressing. Season it to taste.

3 Add the pesto to the vegetables and toss so they are well coated with sauce. Spread them in the baking dish and bake until they are very tender and brown, 40–50 minutes. Decorate the vegetables with herb sprigs, and serve the gratin hot or at room temperature.

Shortcut: Use one of the good ready-made pesto sauces on the market.

Getting Ahead: *Gratin of Summer Vegetables* says Mediterranean to me, a dish that can be baked ahead and keeps happily for a day at room temperature, longer in the refrigerator. Just before serving, you might want to pick up its flavours by sprinkling the gratin with a little more olive oil and some lemon juice or vinegar – in effect a vinaigrette dressing.

On the Side: A gratin of summer vegetables is the perfect accompaniment to grilled fish.

In the Glass: A chilled rosé wine from anywhere you fancy.

Serves 4–6

2 medium courgettes (about 330 g/12 oz)
2 medium yellow or scallop squash (about 330 g/12 oz)
450 g/1 lb tomatoes
2 onions, thinly sliced
salt and pepper

For the pesto
medium bunch (about 40 g/1¹/₂ oz) of mint or other herb
3 garlic cloves, peeled
30 g/1 oz grated Parmesan cheese
2 tablespoons pine nuts
175 ml/6 fl oz olive oil, more for the dish

1.5-litre/2¹/₂-pint gratin or baking dish

food processor

Spring Gratin of Baby Vegetables with Cheese and Mustard Sauce

This spring gratin is multi-purpose for all sorts of vegetables. Here I'm suggesting baby vegetables, but a wide variety of roots and greens do equally well, including celeriac and chopped leaf spinach. Try to include contrasts of colour and texture – carrots are always cheerful, for instance; celery complements other flavours; and it is a poor gratin that has no onion in it at all.

Serves 6 as appetizer, 4 as a light main course

8–10 baby carrots, or 4–5 medium carrots, halved if large (450 g/1 lb)

4–5 baby turnips, halved or quartered depending on size (450 g/1 lb)

8–10 small white onions

3–4 small fennel bulbs, cut in 8 wedges (450 g/1 lb)

4–6 baby courgettes, thickly sliced (450 g/1 lb)

For the cheese and mustard sauce

60 g/2 oz butter, more for the baking dish

30 g/1 oz flour

500 ml/16 fl oz milk, more if needed

salt and pepper

110 g/4 oz grated Gruyère or Cheddar cheese

1^1/$_2$ tablespoons smooth mild or hot Dijon mustard, more to taste

1.5-litre/2^1/$_2$-pint gratin dish, or 4–6 individual dishes

1 Put the carrots in a pan of cold, salted water, cover, bring to the boil and simmer until just tender, 8–10 minutes. Cook the turnips in the same way, allowing 10–15 minutes until just tender. Drain both vegetables and set aside.

2 Bring a pan of salted water to the boil, add the onions and simmer them, uncovered, until just tender, 6–10 minutes. Lift them out with a draining spoon, rinse with cold water and leave to drain thoroughly. Use the same cooking water to cook the fennel and courgette separately in the same way, allowing 5–8 minutes for fennel and 2–3 minutes for courgette.

3 Butter the gratin dish, or individual dishes. Mix all the vegetables and spread them in the dish(es).

4 For the sauce: melt the butter in a saucepan, whisk in the flour and cook for a minute or two. Pour in the milk and bring to the boil, whisking constantly until the sauce thickens. Season and simmer for 2 minutes. Take the sauce from the heat and stir in half the cheese until it melts (do not cook the sauce further or it will cook into strings). Stir in the mustard, taste and adjust the seasoning. It's important not to overheat the mustard as that turns it bitter. The sauce can be spicy, or mild, as you prefer; it should generously coat the back of a spoon but not too thickly so, if necessary, add more milk.

5 Spoon the sauce over the vegetables – they should be completely coated, but still show through a veil of sauce. Sprinkle the remaining cheese on top.

6 To finish: grill the gratin under a medium heat until browned and bubbling around the edges, 8–10 minutes for a large gratin or 6–8 for small ones.

Shortcut: Reduce the number of vegetables to two of contrasting colour and taste.

Getting Ahead: A cinch. Prepare the gratin completely ahead and refrigerate it for up to 24 hours, loosely covered with clingfilm. Reheat it in the oven at 180°C/350°F/Gas Mark 4 for 20 minutes for small dishes or 25–30 minutes for a large dish, then grill it as directed.

On the Side: *Spring Gratin* would be excellent with *Colombian Rice with Vegetables and Coconut Milk* (page 101) or plain boiled rice.

In the Glass: A pleasing white wine that is not too dry, such as an Alsatian-style Riesling or a light Chardonnay.

Winter Gratin Dauphinois

Gratin dauphinois, the chic sister of scalloped potatoes, must be the ultimate comfort food in winter. This superlative version was passed on to me by Chef Fernand Chambrette, a brilliant, cantankerous man whose cooking on a good day was legendary (don't mention the bad days). The chef simmers the potatoes in milk to remove their tannin content, which would otherwise turn them brown and curdle the milk. The milk is then discarded and the potatoes are cooked again, in cream this time, to an inimitable, melting softness.

I really prefer my gratin dauphinois quite plain, but a little bit of garlic can be rubbed around the dish before adding the potatoes, or a few chopped chives can be stirred into them. For a more substantial dish, fry some bacon until crisp and add it to the potatoes before spreading them in the gratin dish. Most importantly, be sure to use a floury potato for gratin dauphinois, such as a Maris Piper, and genuine Gruyère cheese – you'll only need a bit but it makes all the difference.

Serves 6–8

1 kg/2¹/₄ lb potatoes
1.25 litres/2¹/₄ pints milk
375 ml/12 fl oz double cream
375 ml/12 fl oz crème fraîche, or more
  double cream
salt and pepper
large pinch of grated nutmeg
100 g/3¹/₂ oz Gruyère cheese, grated
butter for the baking dish

1 Peel the potatoes and cut them in 6 mm/¹/₄ in slices – they are best sliced evenly using a mandoline slicer if you have one. Add them at once to the milk in a saucepan so they do not discolour. Bring them to the boil and simmer until almost tender, 15–20 minutes (potatoes take longer to cook in milk than in water). Milk and cream scorch easily, so use a heavy pan with the heat just at medium. Stir the potatoes quite often, but take care not to crush them once they start to soften.

2 Drain the potatoes and wipe out the pan. Return them to the pan with the double cream and crème fraîche. Season them to taste with salt, pepper and nutmeg, and bring them just to the boil. Simmer until very tender, stirring occasionally, 10–15 minutes – if the potatoes boil, the cream will curdle.

3 Butter a medium baking dish and spread the potatoes and cream in it – the mixture will be quite sloppy. Sprinkle the top with the grated cheese.

4 To finish: heat the oven to 180°C/350°F/Gas Mark 4. Bake the gratin until very hot and browned on top, 25–30 minutes.

Getting Ahead: The gratin can be made ahead and refrigerated for up to two days. Bake it just before serving.

On the Side: This is a classic with roast lamb and beef steak; as a lighter option, *Vodka and Sesame Salmon* (page 12) contrasts perfectly with the rich and creamy texture of the gratin.

In the Glass: A rich red wine, one of those fruity Merlots from the New World, would be my choice to highlight the potatoes, cream, and cheese. Winter perfection!

TURNIP, JERUSALEM ARTICHOKE OR SWEET POTATO GRATIN DAUPHINOIS

Several root vegetables blend deliciously with potatoes to make unusual first and main course gratins (the starch in potato is always needed to bind the cream). I like to bake mixed vegetable gratins in individual dishes, great for entertaining.

Substitute 450 g/1 lb turnips, jerusalem artichokes or sweet potatoes for half the potatoes. Peel the roots and slice them like the potatoes. Simmer them separately in milk as they will take longer to cook, 20–25 minutes. Then mix the root vegetable with the potatoes and cook both together in the cream as directed in the recipe.

Randall's Pumpkin Flan

The only problem about garden produce is that too much comes all at once, stretching the cook's imagination to the limit. Pumpkin is a notable offender, as is the butternut squash that can be substituted for pumpkin in this recipe. So I'm always happy to pass on ideas like this flan from Chef Randall Price, who has come to Burgundy from Ohio via Washington DC, Budapest and Paris. Randall relishes a challenge and this is just one of his many inspirations. He prefers to bake the pumpkin or butternut in the oven, as he finds it can get very waterlogged if boiled. This recipe doubles easily.

1 To cook the pumpkin: heat the oven to 180°C/350°F/Gas Mark 4. Discard the seeds and fibres and cut the pumpkin in 2–3 pieces, including the rind. Sprinkle with salt, put the pieces in a baking dish with the water for steam and dot the butter over the pumpkin. Cover tightly with foil. Bake in the oven until the pumpkin flesh is very tender, 25–35 minutes.

2 When tender, let the pumpkin cool slightly, then scoop out the flesh and purée it in a processor or blender. Strain it and measure 250 ml/8 fl oz. Leave the oven on. Mix the eggs and yolk in a bowl and stir them into the pumpkin. Stir in the milk and cream. Taste and season the mixture quite highly with nutmeg, salt and pepper.

3 Butter the ramekins, pour in the pumpkin mixture, filling the ramekins to the top. Set the ramekins in a water bath. Bring the water to the boil on top of the stove, transfer the bath to the oven and bake until the flans are set and wobble only slightly in the centre when shaken, 25–30 minutes. A skewer inserted in the centre should come out clean. Meanwhile, braise the leeks.

4 When the flans are set, lift the ramekins from the water bath and let them cool for 5 minutes. Reheat the leeks if necessary and spread them on warm individual plates. Turn out the flans on to the leeks, and serve.

Shortcut: Use canned pumpkin purée. The flan will not be quite as light and fresh-tasting, but good all the same.

Getting Ahead: Bake the flans and sauté the leeks up to a day ahead and keep them tightly covered in the refrigerator. Warm both on top of the stove, using a water bath for the flans.

On the Side: You might want to add some onions and carrots, both cut in quarters and glazed in butter and sugar.

In the Glass: Let's give this recipe an Italian spin with a soft Valpolicella or a more robust Barbaresco from Piedmont. Serve mineral water as an alternative.

Serves 4 as a light meal or 2 as a main course

330 g/12 oz piece of pumpkin
salt and pepper
125 ml/4 fl oz water
15 g/1/2 oz butter, more for ramekins
3 eggs
1 egg yolk
125 ml/4 fl oz milk
125 ml/4 fl oz double cream
grated nutmeg
Braised Leeks (see below)

4 ramekins (125 ml/4 fl oz capacity each)
food processor or blender

BRAISED LEEKS
(Serves 4)
A gentle seasoning of spice is all that is needed for this simple dish. Trim the roots and tops of 900 g/2 lb leeks, leaving some of the green. Halve them lengthwise and cut in 1.25 cm/1/2 in slices. Wash the leeks thoroughly in a bowl of cold water, lift out and drain in a colander. Melt 50 g/11/2 oz butter in a frying pan and stir in 2 teaspoons Chinese five-spice powder or ground allspice and 1 teaspoon salt. Sauté, stirring, for about a minute, then add the leeks. Cover with foil, pressing it on top of the leeks, and add a lid. Cook very gently, stirring occasionally, until meltingly tender, 25–30 minutes.

Wild Mushroom Pie

How is it that the edible mushrooms that grow in so many woods and mountainsides have been ignored for so long? Habits are changing now: I know a restaurateur in northern England who gathers boletus/porcini in the local public park. Over in the USA, in the Appalachians, each spring local mushroom hunters reward lucky cooks with bags of wild morels. You need to know what you are picking, of course – wild mushrooms can be a risk as well as a gourmet prize.

Serves 4–6

110 g/4 oz fresh morels, chanterelles or
    porcini, or 30 g/1 oz dried morels,
    chanterelles or porcini
45 g/1$^{1}/_2$ oz butter
450 g/1 lb button mushrooms, trimmed and
    quartered
salt and pepper
2 tablespoons flour
375 ml/12 fl oz double cream

For the shortcrust pastry
200 g/7 oz plain white flour
$^{3}/_4$ teaspoon salt
45 g/1$^{1}/_2$ oz butter
45 g/1$^{1}/_2$ oz margarine or lard
4 tablespoons cold water, more if needed

shallow 22 cm/9 in pie dish with rim

1 Make the shortcrust pastry (page 165). Wrap it tightly and chill it for 30 minutes or until firm.
2 Pick over and trim the stems of the fresh mushrooms. Soak them for 10–15 minutes in a bowl of water, stirring them occasionally. Lift them out of the water, leaving any sand behind, and drain them. If using dried mushrooms, pour over 500 ml/16 fl oz of boiling water and leave them to soak for 10–15 minutes. Lift out the mushrooms. Strain the liquid though a coffee filter to remove sand and reserve the liquid. Slice the fresh or dried mushrooms.
3 Melt the butter in a medium frying pan, add the button and wild mushrooms, salt and pepper. If you are using dried mushrooms, add the liquid also. Simmer the mushrooms until tender and all the liquid has evaporated, 15–20 minutes. Stir in the flour, add the cream and bring this sauce to the boil, stirring until it thickens. Simmer it for 1 minute, taste for seasoning and pour it into the pie dish. Leave it to cool before covering with the pastry.
4 Roll out the shortcrust pastry and cover the pie dish and filling. Trim the edge, decorate it and slash steam holes in the crust. Chill the pie until the dough is firm, at least 15 minutes. Heat the oven to 190°C/375°F/Gas Mark 5.
5 Bake the pie in the oven until the crust is brown and crisp, 20–25 minutes. Serve the pie warm, not scalding hot.

Shortcut: Use ready-prepared pastry dough for topping the pie.

Getting Ahead: The pie can be prepared up to 24 hours ahead and refrigerated, or frozen; bake it just before serving.

On the Side: I've always found mushrooms and spinach to be natural partners, so you might like to try my *Iranian Spinach*, flavoured with mint and walnuts (see below).

In the Glass: A light red wine such as a Gamay (Beaujolais).

IRANIAN SPINACH
(Serves 4)
In Iran, this spinach is served either hot or as a salad at room temperature, topped with natural yoghurt.

Wash 900 g/2 lb spinach, discarding tough stems, and leave to drain. Heat 2–3 tablespoons olive oil in a large saucepan and fry 1 chopped onion until soft. Stir in 2–3 chopped garlic cloves and fry them for 2 minutes. Pack in the spinach, cover and cook over medium heat until wilted, stirring once or twice, about 5 minutes. Add $^{1}/_2$ cup chopped mint and a little salt and pepper and cook, stirring, until the moisture has evaporated, 3–5 minutes. If you like, stir in a few tablespoons of chopped toasted walnuts (page 166). Taste and adjust the seasoning.

Mexican Stuffed Peppers with Cheese

Like Aubergine Parmigiana *(page 60),* Mexican Stuffed Peppers *are a revelation when made at home. The peppers are lightly crisp yet juicy, and the tomato sauce is perfumed with spice. The chilli of choice for stuffing is the mild poblano, common in Mexico and parts of the US with a sizeable Latin population. A more common alternative is the Anaheim pepper. However, be assured that stuffed peppers are also delicious when made with familiar red or green peppers. Just to pick up the heat when using peppers I include a bit of chopped jalapeño chilli with the cheese.*

Serves 4

8 chilli or 4 peppers (about 750 g/1³/4 lb)

225 g/8 oz piece of mature Cheddar cheese

2 garlic cloves, chopped

3 tablespoons chopped coriander

1 jalapeño pepper, cored, seeded and chopped
  (optional)

500 ml/16 fl oz vegetable oil, more if needed
  (for frying)

For the batter

4 eggs, whisked to mix

75 g/2¹/2 oz plain white flour

salt and pepper

For the tomato broth

450 g/1 lb tomatoes, seeded and chopped, but
  not peeled (page 166)

thick slice of onion, cut in pieces

2 garlic cloves, cut in pieces

2 tablespoons vegetable oil

5 cm/2 in piece of cinnamon stick

2 bay leaves

1 dried chilli pepper

¹/4 teaspoon cloves

salt and pepper

750 ml/1¹/4 pints vegetable stock

food processor or blender

1 To make the tomato broth: purée the tomatoes, onion and garlic in the food processor or blender. Heat the oil in a shallow saucepan and add the tomato purée, cinnamon stick, bay leaves, chilli pepper, cloves, salt and pepper. Fry over quite high heat, stirring often, until the tomato mixture thickens so it just falls easily from a spoon, 12–15 minutes. Discard the cinnamon stick, bay leaves and chilli pepper, stir in the stock and bring the broth just to the boil. Taste, adjust the seasoning and set it aside.

2 To peel the peppers: heat the grill. Brush a grill rack with oil, add the peppers and grill them about 7.5 cm/3 in from the heat, turning them until the skin chars and bursts, 10–12 minutes. Put them in a plastic bag to retain steam as this helps loosen the skins. Leave them to cool. Peel the peppers, leaving the stems attached. Carefully make a slit in the side of each, stopping short of the stem and pointed ends. With the tip of a knife or your fingers, pull out the cores and seeds.

3 Cut the cheese into eight sticks just shorter than the peppers. Whisk the eggs in a shallow bowl until frothy. In another shallow bowl mix the garlic, coriander and jalapeño (if using). Dip the cheese sticks first in egg, then in the chopped garlic mixture, and insert them in the peppers. Reserve the remaining egg.

4 To coat the peppers: mix the flour with salt and pepper and spread it on a plate. Lifting the peppers by the stems, coat them first in flour, patting with your hands to discard the excess. Transfer them to a plate. Have the plate of remaining egg ready.

5 Heat the oil for frying in a deep frying pan – there should be enough to make a 2 cm/³/4 in layer. When a drop of egg sizzles briskly in the fat, dip a pepper into the egg to coat both sides and lower the pepper carefully into the fat. Repeat with remaining peppers. Fry them until golden brown, 3–5 minutes, turning them once. Drain them on paper towels.

6 Reheat the tomato broth. Set two fried chilli peppers or one pepper in each of four soup bowls, spoon around the broth and serve at once while hot and crisp.

Getting Ahead: The tomato broth can be made in advance and the peppers can be stuffed ready for coating up to 24 hours ahead. Keep them in the refrigerator. Coat the peppers in batter and fry them just before serving.

On the Side: Spanish rice or refried beans.

In the Glass: Chilled Mexican beer.

Colombian Rice with Vegetables and Coconut Milk

One of the joys of travel is to come across dishes that at first sight seem quite strange, and that then turn out to be childishly simple. I was puzzled, in the Colombian city of Cartegena, to be served dish after dish with a wonderful colour and perfume. Guiso *turned out to be the secret, a seasoning mixture of vegetables cooked slowly in annatto-infused oil. Annato is a seed that colours food bright yellow-orange (it is often used in cheese). Rice cooked with coconut milk and seasoned with* guiso *is almost a Colombian national dish.*

Serves 4–6 as a first course

300 g/11 oz long grain rice

For the *guiso*

2 tablespoons annatto-infused oil, or
  vegetable oil (see below)

3 garlic cloves, chopped

3 spring onions, white and pale green only,
  finely chopped

2 plum tomatoes, peeled, seeded, and
  chopped (page 166)

1 small green pepper or mild chilli pepper,
  cored, seeded, and finely chopped

1 red onion, finely chopped

425 ml/14 fl oz canned unsweetened
  coconut milk

300 ml/10 fl oz water

2 teaspoons salt

3 coriander sprigs

1 Put the rice in a sieve and rinse it under cold running water. Stir and turn the rice with your hands until the water running through is clear, not cloudy – this removes excess starch. Shake off excess water and leave the rice to drain. Make the annatto-infused oil, if using.

2 Prepare the *guiso*: heat the oil in a heavy-based saucepan over medium heat. Add the garlic and cook until fragrant, about 30 seconds. Add the spring onions, tomatoes, pepper and onion and cook, stirring often, until the sauce is thick and almost dry, about 10 minutes.

3 Add the rice and cook, stirring constantly, until it is lightly toasted, about 1 minute. Stir in the coconut milk, water and salt. Add the coriander sprigs and bring the rice to the boil. Simmer uncovered and without stirring until the liquid barely covers the rice, about 10 minutes. Reduce the heat to low, cover, and cook without stirring or lifting the cover until the rice is tender, 15–20 minutes. Taste to test when it is done, then remove from the heat and leave the rice in a warm place so the grains contract a bit, 8–10 minutes. Discard the coriander sprigs, fluff the rice with a fork, taste and adjust the seasoning.

Getting Ahead: Copy Colombian cooks and make *guiso* in large quantities. It keeps in the refrigerator for at least two weeks, and a spoonful or two adds great character to soups and stews. With *guiso* ready, all you need do here is cook the rice.

On the Side: To make this rice a delicious main course, just before letting it rest in a warm place, scatter 450 g/1 lb raw peeled prawns on top; the heat from the rice will steam them to perfection.

In the Glass: We're in the tropics here, so cold beer would almost certainly be the local choice.

ANNATO-INFUSED OIL
(Makes 250 ml/8 fl oz)
Annato, often called by the Spanish name *achiote*, is popular in Latin American dishes such as Mexican *homitos* of braised pork with vegetables.
    Put 250 ml/8 fl oz vegetable oil with 40 g/1½ oz annato seeds in a small saucepan. Heat over medium heat until the oil begins to barely simmer and the oil turns reddish-orange, 8–10 minutes. Do not boil the oil as this will make it bitter. Let the oil cool slightly, then strain through a fine-mesh sieve, discarding the seeds. Store the oil in an airtight container in the refrigerator for up to a month.

Red-wine Risotto *is a sumptuous dish – dark, rich and an instant invitation to feasting. When I first tasted it, I couldn't wait to get home and try making it, and risotto made with red wine has remained a favourite ever since. For a hearty main course, I add squid or prawns, or chunky wild mushrooms or glazed shallots for a vegetarian option.* Red-wine Risotto, *served plain, also makes a superb first course – with just a bowl of grated Parmesan for sprinkling.*

Round-grain rice is essential for risotto – a variety such as arborio, carnaroli *or one of their cousins will absorb four times its own volume of liquid, gathering flavour all the time until the grains soften and thicken to that creamy texture we all so enjoy. The red wine is equally important: a cheerful, no-name red with plenty of guts, something fruity made last year, would be my choice as a light wine simply fades away in the pan. Use a mild stock so the wine is not overwhelmed.*

Red-wine Risotto

(Serves 6 as a first course, 4 as a main course)

500 ml/16 fl oz chicken or vegetable stock, more
    if needed
90 g/3 oz butter
1 medium onion, chopped
salt and pepper
200 g/7 oz round-grain risotto rice
500 ml/16 fl oz red wine
grated Parmesan, for serving

Heat the stock in a saucepan and keep it warm at the side of the stove. Melt half the butter in another saucepan or casserole, add the onion with salt and pepper and sauté for 5–7 minutes until soft, but not browned. Stir in the rice and sauté it, stirring constantly, until it absorbs the butter, about 2 minutes.

Stir in half the wine with a little salt and pepper and simmer, stirring, until the rice starts to dry, 5–7 minutes. Add a couple of ladlefuls of hot stock and continue simmering, stirring gently but constantly. When the rice dries again and needs more liquid, add the remaining wine.

Continue cooking, stirring all the time and adding more stock in batches. At the end of cooking, the rice should be tender, still slightly *al dente* (chewy) and creamy from the starch that has begun to leach from the grains. This will take 25–35 minutes – don't hesitate to use plenty of stock. I like my risotto very soft, scarcely holding any shape, so when the wine is finished I keep adding stock to achieve the right consistency.

Take the risotto from the heat, add the remaining butter in pieces, and stir it into the rice as it melts. This process marries all the flavours together. Taste and adjust the seasoning. Serve the risotto in shallow bowls or on deep plates. It is best eaten at once, though it can be kept warm for a few minutes. If necessary, soften it with a little more stock just before serving.

FLAVOURINGS FOR RED-WINE RISOTTO

Spicy Greens

The darker the greens, the more eye-catching is this risotto. Rocket, sprouting broccoli, Savoy cabbage or spinach are all good choices.

Discard any tough stems from 675 g/1 1/2 lb greens, wash the leaves and any florets and drain the greens in a colander. Coarsely chop them. Heat 3 tablespoons olive oil in a large frying pan, add 1 lightly crushed garlic clove and sauté it just until fragrant, about 30 seconds. Discard the garlic and add the greens, salt and pepper. Cover and cook gently until tender, stirring occasionally, 5–10 minutes depending on age and type of greens. Taste, adjust the seasoning and keep warm. When the risotto is ready, stir in the greens. Alternatively, spoon the risotto into bowls and pile the greens on top for contrast of colour. Serve a bowl of grated Parmesan cheese separately.

Mushroom

As a warm first-course salad, serve these mushrooms on a bed of rocket or baby spinach.

Trim 450–675 g/1–1 1/2 lb wild or cultivated mushrooms, and wipe them to remove earth. Quarter or cut them in chunks. Heat 2 tablespoons each of olive oil and butter in a saucepan and fry 4 sliced shallots with salt and pepper until soft, 2–3 minutes. Stir in 3 chopped garlic cloves and heat for 30 seconds. Add the mushrooms with 3–4 sprigs of thyme, salt and pepper and fry them, stirring often, until they are tender and all liquid has evaporated, 5–8 minutes depending on the type of mushroom. Take from the heat and discard the thyme sprigs. Taste, adjust the seasoning and set the mushrooms aside. When the risotto is ready, stir in the mushrooms with 3–4 tablespoons chopped parsley. Heat gently for 1–2 minutes.

Caramelized Shallots

Try stirring these caramelized shallots into cooked kidney beans, preferably cannellini, and you'll have a real treat.

Melt 30 g/1 oz butter in a saucepan and add 20 peeled shallots – they should all touch the base of the pan. Sprinkle with salt and pepper and brown them, stirring, for 5–7 minutes. Sprinkle over 2 tablespoons sugar and cook for 1–2 minutes longer to caramelize them. Deglaze the pan with 3 tablespoons red wine vinegar, stirring to dissolve the pan juices. Then add 250 ml/8 fl oz vegetable stock and bring to the boil. Cover and simmer, stirring often, until the shallots are very brown and meltingly tender, 20–30 minutes. Set them aside and cook the risotto. When it is ready, stir in the shallots.

TIPS FOR RISOTTO

The process of stirring in butter – and sometimes Parmesan – at the end of cooking is known as *mantecare*.

A more traditional risotto is made with white rather than red wine. In this recipe, use a medium-dry white wine such as Soave. Reduce the amount of wine by half, substituting more stock.

Arborio is the classic rice for risotto, and the most plentifully produced. The kernels have a distinctive white spot on them. *Vialone Nano* is another appropriate favourite, a shorter grain than *arborio*. *Carnaroli* is scarce and more expensive, but cooks to be perfectly tender.

When I was a child, a baked egg fresh from the farm was my standard supper. My mother would hide secrets underneath it – a few fresh peas, a bit of smoked haddock left from breakfast, or some crispy croûtons fried in bacon fat.

Serves 4 as an appetizer or 2 as a main course

4 eggs
butter for the dish
chosen filling (below)
salt and pepper
4 tablespoons double cream (optional)

4 ramekins (175–250 ml/6–8 fl oz capacity) or 2 gratin
    dishes (15 cm/6 in)

Heat the oven to 190°C/375°F/Gas Mark 5 and butter the ramekins or gratin dishes. Spread your chosen filling in the bottom, making a shallow well in the centre to hold the egg(s). Sprinkle the well with salt and pepper (if the eggs are seasoned on top, they will be spotty when baked). Break the eggs into the well, and spoon cream on top if using.

For ramekins: set the ramekins in a water bath and bring to the boil on top of the stove. Transfer to the oven and cook until the whites are almost set and the yolks are still soft, 5–8 minutes. For gratin dishes: set the dishes on a baking sheet and bake until the egg whites are almost set, 8–12 minutes. The cooking time depends very much on the thickness of the ramekins.

FILLINGS FOR BAKED EGGS

Onion Filling (*Lyonnaise*)

The citizens of Lyon have always loved onions! Melt 30 g/1 oz butter and sauté 2 very thinly sliced onions with salt and pepper, stirring occasionally, until very brown. Stir in 1 tablespoon chopped parsley and spread the onions in ramekins or gratin dishes.

For croûtons: discard the crusts from 2 slices of white bread and cut them in cubes. Melt another 30 g/1 oz butter and fry the bread until brown, stirring constantly so the croûtons brown evenly. Spoon them on to the onions. Top the eggs with cream before baking.

Garden Filling (*Jardinière*)

The more colourful the vegetables, the better.

Finely dice 1 medium potato, 1 carrot and 1 celery stick. Heat 30 g/1 oz butter and sauté the vegetables with salt and pepper until tender and lightly browned. Then stir in 1 tablespoon of chopped tarragon, thyme or sage and spread in the dishes. A topping of cream is optional.

Cheese Filling

Here again, eggs benefit from crispy croûtons.

Make the croûtons as for the onion filling. Spread them in the ramekins or gratin dishes and top with 2 tablespoons grated Gruyère or Cheddar cheese. Add the eggs, top with cream and sprinkle with 2 tablespoons more cheese.

Mushroom Filling

Made with wild mushrooms, eggs are a gourmet dish.

Trim and thinly slice 4–5 button mushrooms (60 g/2 oz). Heat 30 g/1 oz butter and fry a chopped garlic clove just until fragrant, about 30 seconds. Add the mushrooms with nutmeg, salt and pepper and sauté, stirring, until they are tender and their liquid has evaporated. Stir in 1 tablespoon chopped parsley and spread in the ramekins or gratin dishes. Top the eggs with cream before baking.

Pepper, Tomato, and Onion Filling (*Basquaise*)

A Basque favourite. A type of spicy red pepper, called the *espelette*, is characteristic of Basque cooking. Use a dried pinch or two of it here if you find it.

Heat 2 tablespoons olive oil in a frying pan and fry a sliced onion until just browned. Stir in a cored, seeded and very thinly sliced pepper with 2 chopped garlic cloves, salt and pepper. Sauté, stirring, until the pepper is wilted. Stir in a peeled, seeded and chopped tomato (page 166) and continue cooking until most of the moisture has evaporated. Spread in the ramekins or gratin dishes. A topping of cream is optional.

TIPS FOR BAKED EGGS

A single egg does well as a first course when baked in a ramekin. For a main course, spread the garnish down in an individual gratin dish, making hollows for two to three eggs.
Note that baked eggs will continue to cook in the heat of the dishes, so don't let them get over done. The cooking time will vary with the type of dish you use and the quantity of filling.
Leftovers, such as sautéed vegetables, make an easy filling. It's up to you and your creativity!

The simpler the sauce for pasta, the better it seems to be, full of freshness and life. After spending a summer on the island of Elba, our daughter Emma taught me perhaps the quickest idea of all. She shreds fresh herbs, chops a tomato and puts them in a big bowl with plenty of ground black pepper. Very hot olive oil is poured on top, the hot pasta is added, tossed and eccolo! As for the other recipes here, it is hard to imagine pasta without the tomato. My trio of tomato sauces ranges from an uncooked coulis to a dark, mysterious brew which, it seems to me, must date from Roman times, before European pasta was even born.

Fresh Tomato Coulis

(Makes 500 ml/16 fl oz coulis, enough for 450 g/1 lb pasta)
This 'sauce' is not cooked at all. When served with pasta, the coulis is usually spooned on top of the hot pasta rather than mixed with it.

450 g/1 lb tomatoes
salt and pepper
2 tablespoons chopped fresh basil, oregano or flatleaf
   parsley
juice of 1/2 lemon
pinch of sugar

Peel, seed, and chop the tomatoes (page 166). Stir in a little salt and pepper and leave to stand in a colander for 30 minutes to drain excess juice. Mix the tomatoes with the herb, lemon juice and sugar. Taste and adjust the seasoning.

Venetian Tomato Sauce

(Makes 500 ml/16 fl oz, enough for 450 g/1 lb pasta)
At first I was appalled to hear a Venetian chef admit to using tinned tomatoes in his pasta sauce. But he was right – the result is delicious, and so easy that you'll have spaghetti on the table in 10 minutes. The sauce is quite oily, just right for pasta; when I use it for other dishes, I cut the oil by half.

250 ml/8 fl oz tinned tomatoes
3 medium fresh tomatoes
several rosemary, sage and thyme sprigs
125 ml/4 fl oz olive oil
2–3 peeled garlic cloves
3–4 tablespoons shredded basil

Drain and chop the tinned tomatoes. Peel, seed and chop the fresh tomatoes (page 166). Crush the rosemary, sage and thyme with a rolling pin to bruise them and add to the oil and garlic in a small pan. Heat until the oil is very fragrant, about 3 minutes. Meanwhile, combine the canned and fresh tomatoes in a saucepan with the basil. Strain the hot oil over the tomatoes. Stir until mixed, taste it and adjust the seasoning. Toss the sauce with the hot pasta, or if serving it separately, heat it 1–2 minutes before serving.

Cooked Tomato Sauce

(Makes 500 ml/16 fl oz, enough for 450 g/1 lb pasta)
This tomato sauce is thoroughly cooked, concentrated and chunky, so just a few spoonfuls go a long way for pasta, pizza or grilled fish. Unlike uncooked tomato sauces, it keeps well in the refrigerator for up to a week.

2–3 tablespoons olive oil
2 onions, chopped
salt and pepper
175 ml/6 fl oz dry red or white wine
900 g/2 lb plum tomatoes
3–4 thyme or oregano sprigs, chopped
2 tablespoons chopped basil or oregano

Heat the oil and stir in the onion with salt and pepper and sauté until very soft, 5–7 minutes. Add the wine and boil until reduced by half. Meanwhile, peel, seed and chop the tomatoes (page 166). Stir them into the onions with the thyme or oregano, salt and pepper. Simmer the sauce uncovered, stirring often, until it is thick and concentrated, 30–45 minutes. Stir in the basil or oregano, taste, and adjust the seasoning.

TIPS ON COOKING PASTA

Pasta portions: 450 g/1 lb of fresh or dried pasta serves 6–8 as an appetizer or 4 as a main course when garnished with a simple sauce. If a filling is rich or elaborate, use less pasta.
To boil pasta: Allow 5 litres/8 3/4 pints water for the first 450 g/1 lb of pasta, and increase by 1 litre/1 3/4 pints for each additional 225 g/ 8 oz pasta. A tablespoon of salt is needed for 450 g/1 lb pasta and should be added after the water has come to the boil. A tablespoon of oil added to the water will help keep pasta from sticking together and the water from boiling over. When the water boils, add the pasta. Dried long pasta, such as spaghetti, must be bent slowly into the water until completely covered. Fresh pasta cooks very quickly, so test as soon as it comes back to the boil. Thin dried pasta should be tested after 3 minutes' boiling, larger shapes can take up to 12 minutes. For dried commercial pasta, be sure to look on the package. Times can vary greatly with the age and dryness of pasta, so you should always apply the famous *al dente* test to tell when it is done. Fish out a strand and bite it – it should be firm and slightly chewy but not hard and floury. Over done, pasta is an abomination.

I am lucky when it comes to parties. So many entertainments have been given in our 300-year-old house that I don't have to think about the ambience. The welcome is ready-made. So my first concern is to choose food that is a treat, for me as cook, as well as for the guests. Simple cooking is the key – warm, welcoming dishes that have a strong sense of place. An example is *Salmon in Red-wine Sauce*, a Burgundian recipe that is beloved of our neighbours and makes good use of our local Pinot Noir. France produces the very best poultry, so you'll find recipes here for duck, goose and turkey.

Next, I look for amusement, such as parcels of wonton that conceal a happy surprise. A traditional game pie with its lid of puff pastry offers the same sense of anticipation, as well as tempting aromas when the crust is cut. I enjoy a bit of a twist, such as the sweet chilli sauce accompanying scallops, and the dried apricots and prunes alongside a luscious brown roast of veal. As for fantasy, you may think raspberries in the whisky sauce for pigeon is going too far – but it's good!

A party is the moment to step back from the speed and pressure of everyday cooking and take some time. That means planning ahead, choosing dishes that can be prepared at least partly in advance. I'm an old hand at simmering a sauce the day before, or shaping parcels ready to bake, as you'll see in 'Getting Ahead'. However a special part of entertaining at home is the chance to serve dishes straight from the stove – freshly steamed dumplings, for example, or a festive bird roasted until crisp and fragrant. Guests love to share in all of this, so a pre-dinner party in the kitchen is often part of the action.

Last, but certainly not least, comes the presentation. A plain roast bird will be transformed by a bevy of accompanying vegetables on a grand platter. A background of greens on each serving plate can display a main ingredient to perfection. Fancy garnishes, however, I leave to restaurant chefs. For me, more is often less, and a simple plate, a few leaves or a slice of lemon concentrates attention on the food itself. A party is a theatre, with the cook as producer and the dishes as stars.

Perfect for Parties

Sole Véronique

For sheer romance it's hard to rival Sole Véronique. The gentle sweetness of green grapes with sole, the finest of all white fish, is bound to draw a big smile when guests start tasting. Escoffier himself would have approved of this classic velouté sauce, in which white wine is used to lightly simmer the grapes and then poach the fish. The concentrated essence from cooking is thickened with a roux and enriched with egg yolk and cream. Clearly the wine is key and I've found that the herbal notes and touch of acid in Sauvignon Blanc are a perfect match. Lemon sole, grey sole or flounder can be substituted for Dover sole.

Serves 4

170 g/6 oz seedless green grapes

250 ml/8 fl oz medium-dry white wine

500 ml/16 fl oz fish stock

2 shallots, chopped

4 plump Dover sole fillets each weighing about
   110 g/4 oz, skinned

For the sauce

30 g/1 oz butter, more for the pan

2 tablespoons flour

2 egg yolks

125 ml/4 fl oz crème fraîche or double cream

squeeze of lemon juice

salt and white pepper

large frying pan

large baking dish or 4 heatproof gratin dishes
   or plates

1 Put the grapes in a pan with the wine and simmer for 1–2 minutes until lightly cooked (do not overcook them or they will burst). Lift them out with a draining spoon and set them aside. Add the stock to the wine in the pan and boil until reduced by half, 8–10 minutes.

2 Meanwhile, butter a heavy frying pan and sprinkle with the shallots. Cut the sole fillets in half lengthwise to make eight fillets. Wash and dry them on paper towels and fold them in three, skinned-side inwards and with the ends tucked under. Set them in the pan.

3 Pour over the reduced wine and stock, cover with a disc of non-stick baking paper and then cover with the lid and bring to the boil. Lower the heat and poach until the fish starts to flake when tested with a fork but is still very firm in the centre, 2–3 minutes. Let the stock cool slightly and then, with a draining spoon, transfer the fish to a plate. Then boil the cooking liquid for 2 minutes or until reduced to about 250 ml/8 fl oz.

4 For the sauce: melt the butter in a pan, whisk in the flour and cook for $1/2$–1 minute. Strain in the cooking liquid and bring the sauce to the boil, whisking constantly until it thickens. Simmer until it coats a spoon, 1–2 minutes.

5 Make the liaison to enrich the sauce: mix the egg yolks and crème fraîche or cream in a small bowl. Whisk in some of the hot sauce. Add this mixture back to the sauce and reheat, stirring, until it thickens slightly. Take care not to boil the sauce at this stage or it will curdle. Take it off the heat and stir in the grapes and juice, and any liquid that has come from the fish. Add a squeeze of lemon juice, taste and adjust the seasoning of the sauce with salt and white pepper.

6 Dry the folded fish fillets on paper towels and set them in one large or four individual gratin dishes. Coat them with the sauce.

7 Just before serving, heat the grill to its highest setting. Set the serving dish(es) as near to the grill as you can and brown until the sauce is glazed, 2–3 minutes. It's very important to glaze the sauce as quickly as possible or it may overcook and curdle. Serve at once.

Shortcut: Omit the egg yolk and cream liaison. The sauce will be less rich, and also more stable with no danger of curdling.

Getting Ahead: The fish can be cooked and the sauce made up to 4 hours ahead. Keep them covered in the refrigerator. Shortly before serving, warm the fish, covered in foil, in a very low oven. Reheat the sauce, add the egg yolk and cream liaison, and finish the recipe as directed.

On the Side: Small boiled potatoes in their skins, or small potatoes that have been peeled, cut in neat olive shapes (technically known as 'turned'), and then steamed. *Sole Véronique* plays on pastel shades and asks for pretty heatproof plates as background to the individual gratin dishes.

In the Glass: Nothing works as well with *Sole Véronique* as a fine Riesling.

Grilled Scallops with Sweet Chilli Sauce

Fusion is a controversial word in my kitchen. All too often it means confusion, a muddle of ingredients thrown on to a plate with no reason or structure. But on occasion, Asian spice and western technique – here, the presentation with watercress and crème fraîche – combine with brilliance; this is one of them. Grilled Scallops with Sweet Chilli Sauce *is quick to make, easy to prepare ahead and stunning on the plate.*

1 For the sweet chilli sauce: combine the lemon grass, garlic, chilli, ginger and coriander in the food processor and work them to a coarse paste.

2 To make the caramel: in a small, heavy pan gently heat the sugar and water until the sugar dissolves, stirring occasionally. Have a large bowl of cold water ready. Boil the syrup without stirring until it cooks to a light golden caramel. Lower the heat and continue cooking the syrup for a few more seconds to very deep golden. Plunge the base of the pan in cold water to stop the caramel cooking. Add the vinegar and heat, stirring, until the caramel dissolves (stand back as the vinegar will sting your eyes). Stir in the lemon grass and chilli paste, then the fish sauce and tamari or soy. Set the sauce aside.

3 To cook the scallops: heat the grill and brush the rack with sesame oil. Discard the small inedible ligament at the side of the white meat from the scallops, pat and dry them on paper towels. Brush the scallops with more oil and sprinkle with salt and pepper. Grill the scallops about 5 cm/2 in from the heat until they start to brown but are still translucent in the centre, 1–2 minutes on each side. Arrange a bed of watercress on four individual plates, add the hot scallops and top with a spoonful of crème fraîche. Drizzle them generously with sweet chilli sauce and serve at once.

Getting Ahead: Make the sauce ahead – it will keep for up to a week in the refrigerator – and grill the scallops at the last minute.

On the Side: Let's go Asian with steamed rice or rice noodles.

In the Glass: A feisty white with body and just a touch of sugar. I would explore the hot-climate Chardonnays from California or Australia.

Serves 6

18–24 large sea scallops (about 1 kg/2^{1}/$_{4}$ lb)

dark sesame oil, for brushing

salt and pepper

bunch of watercress, washed and dried

125 ml/4 fl oz crème fraîche (see below)

For the sweet chilli sauce

1 lemon grass stem, peeled and cut in pieces

2 garlic cloves, peeled

1 small red chilli, more to taste, stemmed, seeded and coarsely chopped

5 cm/2 in piece of fresh root ginger, sliced

3–4 tablespoons chopped coriander

75 g/2^{1}/$_{2}$ oz sugar

60 ml/2 fl oz water

60 ml/2 fl oz cider vinegar

2 tablespoons Thai fish sauce (*nam pla*)

1 tablespoon tamari or soy sauce

food processor, preferably small

CRÈME FRAÎCHE
(Makes 1 litre/1^{3}/$_{4}$ pints, serves 6–8)

This thick French cream has a slightly tart flavour that's particularly good in sauces. It is easy to make using high-fat double cream and cultured buttermilk labelled 'active'.

Stir together in a saucepan 750 ml/1^{1}/$_{4}$ pints double cream, 250 ml/8 fl oz buttermilk, and the juice of 1 lemon. Heat gently, stirring, until just below body temperature. Pour the cream into a container and partly cover it. Keep it in a warm place until it thickens and develops a slightly tart flavour; this will take anywhere from 12 to 24 hours depending on the buttermilk culture and the temperature of the cream.

Salmon in Red-wine Sauce

Burgundians have long enjoyed breaking the convention that only white wine is right with fish, and how right they are! The local meurette *red-wine sauce, made with Pinot Noir, is light in texture with the deep rich flavours of bacon, onion and mushroom. Paired with fish it's a revelation, the perfect brunch on a chilly day. The fish is actually poached in wine, giving it an odd purple colour – don't worry, it is hidden beneath the splendid sauce. You'll need a light Pinot Noir or Merlot, or possibly a Beaujolais. Also I add a secret ingredient – a nut of chocolate to round out the wine.*

Serves 6

1 kg/2¼ lb salmon fillet with skin

1 bottle (750 ml) light red wine, such as
   Beaujolais

500 ml/16 fl oz veal or chicken stock, or water

1 onion, thinly sliced

1 carrot, thinly sliced

1 celery stick, thinly sliced

1 garlic clove, crushed

1 bouquet garni

½ teaspoon peppercorns

hazelnut-sized piece of dark or unsweetened
   chocolate

1 tablespoon chopped parsley, for sprinkling

For the garnish

30 g/1 oz butter

110 g/4 oz bacon, diced

110 g/4 oz mushrooms, sliced

16–20 baby onions, peeled

salt and pepper

For the kneaded butter

30 g/1 oz butter, softened

30 g/1 oz flour

Pictured, page 7

1 Cut the fish into six portions, rinse and dry them on paper towels. Bring the wine and stock or water to the boil in a sauté pan. Add the fish, cover and poach just until it flakes easily, 2–3 minutes. Lift it out with a draining spoon and set aside. Add the onion, carrot, celery, garlic, bouquet garni and peppercorns to the poaching liquid and simmer until reduced to 575 ml/1 pint, 15–20 minutes.

2 Meanwhile, prepare the garnish: melt half the butter in a pan and fry the bacon until browned, 3–5 minutes. Transfer it to a bowl with a draining spoon. Add the mushrooms, fry them for 2–3 minutes until tender and any liquid has evaporated, and put them with the bacon. Melt the remaining butter, add the baby onions to the pan, season and sauté them gently until brown and tender, 12–15 minutes. Shake the pan from time to time so they colour evenly. Drain off any fat, return the mushrooms and bacon to the pan and set aside.

3 For the kneaded butter: mash the butter with a fork and work in the flour to form a soft paste. When the poaching liquid has reduced, bring it to the boil. Add the butter piece by piece to the boiling sauce, whisking constantly so the butter melts and thickens it evenly. Add enough butter so the sauce lightly coats a spoon – it may not all be needed. Whisk in the chocolate. Strain the sauce over the garnish, pressing the vegetables into the sieve to extract all the liquid and flavour. Reheat the sauce, taste and adjust the seasoning.

4 Just before serving: return the salmon to the sauce and heat gently for 1–2 minutes. Put the fish on six warm serving plates, spoon over the sauce and garnish, and sprinkle with parsley.

Getting Ahead: If you are prepared to devote two bottles of wine to this recipe, the sauce and garnish can be prepared 24 hours ahead and refrigerated. Cook the fish just before serving, using a second bottle of wine (you can use the leftover poaching liquid to make fish soup). Alternatively, the whole recipe can be prepared up to 4 hours ahead and reheated to serve.

On the Side: Serve *Salmon in Red-wine Sauce* with fresh noodles or small boiled potatoes to absorb the splendid sauce.

In the Glass: Given the luxury of this dish, a Pinot Noir is surely mandatory at table.

Steamed Prawn Dumplings with Sesame Sauce

These Cantonese dumplings are intended as a first course, but I can down half a dozen as lunch, no problem. You can make other fillings by substituting chicken breast or pork for the prawns. Soft goats' cheese crushed with chopped herbs is good, too, though not at all traditional.

Makes about 40 dumplings, to serve 6–8 as an appetizer

225 g/8 oz raw prawns

6 water chestnuts, cut into pieces

2 tablespoons diced pork fat or bacon

1 tablespoon dark sesame oil

2 teaspoons dry sherry

1 teaspoon soy sauce

1 teaspoon sugar

40 wonton wrappers

For the sesame dipping sauce

6 spring onions, white and green parts, trimmed
    and finely sliced

7.5 cm/3 in piece of fresh root ginger, peeled and
    finely chopped

1 tablespoon dark sesame oil

2 teaspoons rice or wine vinegar

1 teaspoon salt

1 teaspoon white pepper

150 ml/5 fl oz groundnut oil

food processor

1 For the dipping sauce: combine the spring onions, ginger, sesame oil, vinegar, salt and pepper in a bowl. Heat the groundnut oil until almost smoking – a drop of water should sizzle at once. Whisk the hot oil into the flavourings. Pour the sauce into serving bowls for dipping and leave to cool.

2 Shell and de-vein the prawns and cut them into pieces. Put them in the food processor with the water chestnuts, pork fat or bacon, sesame oil, sherry, soy sauce and sugar. Work until very finely chopped and the mixture comes away from sides of the bowl in a ball, $1/2$–1 minute. Heat some water in the bottom of a steamer.

3 To shape the dumplings: spread half the wrappers on a work surface and wet the edges of each one with your finger dipped in water. Set a teaspoon of the filling in the centre. For square wrappers, fold two edges together to form a triangle and seal by pinching the edges together. Wet the corners at the base of the triangle and pinch them together. For round wrappers, fold them in a half moon and pinch the edges to seal.

4 Arrange the dumplings in the steamer without overlapping. Cover and steam them for 3–4 minutes. Turn them over and continue steaming until they are tender and the filling is firm, 3–4 minutes longer. Repeat with the remaining dumplings and filling, adding hot water to the steamer as needed between batches. Serve the dumplings hot, with dipping sauce separately.

Getting Ahead: The dipping sauce keeps well for two days in the refrigerator and the flavour mellows. The dumplings can be shaped up to 8 hours ahead and kept in the refrigerator covered with a damp towel, ready to be steamed at the last minute.

On the Side: Set the dumplings on a bed of shredded lettuce, with some sliced cucumber dressed with white wine vinegar, salt and pepper.

In the Glass: At my place it would be a small carafe of sake, hot or chilled depending on the heat of the day.

Moroccan Crown Roast of Turkey

This is an old favourite of mine, first encountered at the Moroccan embassy in Washington, where we all sat on cushions around the turkey, pulling off pieces of meat with our fingers in traditional style. Here I've adapted the idea to a crown roast of turkey, which has the legs and backbone removed, leaving you just the white breast meat to cook on the bone so it stays juicy. The roast is done more quickly than a whole bird and there are no tough legs to cope with. The golden honey and nut finish blends wonderfully well with the delicate meat, and also forms a tempting gravy.

1 Heat the oven to 180°C/350°F/Gas Mark 4. Spread sesame seeds and almonds in a shallow pan and dry-roast them on top of the stove, shaking the pan occasionally, for 4–5 minutes or until golden. Set them aside to cool.
2 In a small bowl, mix the cinnamon, coriander, cumin, ginger, cloves, salt and pepper. Rinse the turkey roast and dry it with paper towels, then rub the upper surface and the cavity with the spice mixture.
3 Put the turkey, breastbone upwards, in a small roasting pan and spread the skin with the butter. Melt the honey with half the stock and pour it over the turkey. Roast in the heated oven for 1–1¹/₄ hours, basting often to keep the meat moist. When the honey glaze starts to brown, add the remaining stock as the honey topping scorches easily. If the pan dries, add more stock, and if the turkey browns too much, cover it loosely with foil.
4 After an hour, take the turkey from the oven and strain the pan juices into a small saucepan. Skim off any fat and boil the juices until reduced to about 250 ml/8 fl oz of glaze. Stir in the toasted sesame seeds and almonds. Return the turkey to the roasting pan, spread the glaze over the top and continue roasting, basting every 3–5 minutes, until the skin is dark golden brown and crisp, 8–10 minutes – watch carefully as it colours quickly. The roast is done if it feels very firm when you pinch the breast between finger and thumb. When pierced with a fork, the juice should run clear, not pink, and a meat thermometer stuck in the thickest part should register 80°C/175°F.
5 Transfer the turkey to a platter and arrange your chosen accompaniments around it – the more colourful they are, the better.

Shortcut: Buy a boneless turkey breast instead of crown roast and you can probably cut the cooking time to 45 minutes.

Getting Ahead: If you want to cook this turkey ahead, I would not try to reheat it as it will be very dry. Instead, slice it to serve at room temperature, when the spices and nuts really shine. Saffron couscous and an orange salad will be just right on the side at room temperature, too.

On the Side: I like to pursue the Moroccan theme with couscous, coloured golden with saffron, or you can serve the turkey with your favourite vegetable accompaniments. A salad of sliced oranges adds just the right note – arrange the slices in overlapping layers with sliced sweet onions or tomatoes, top with lemon vinaigrette.

In the Glass: In Morocco, a glass of pleasant, fruity red wine would accompany the turkey, with mint tea to round off the meal. If children are at the table you may prefer to serve mineral water.

Serves 4–6

1 tablespoon sesame seeds

60 g/2 oz finely chopped blanched almonds

2 teaspoons ground cinnamon

1 teaspoon ground coriander

1 teaspoon ground cumin

1 teaspoon ground ginger

¹/₂ teaspoon ground cloves

¹/₂ teaspoon salt

¹/₂ teaspoon ground pepper

2.25 kg/5 lb crown roast of turkey

30 g/1 oz butter, softened

3 heaped tablespoons honey

250 ml/8 fl oz chicken stock, more if needed

Chicken in a Crispy Cracker with Mushrooms

A touch of fantasy never goes amiss at a party, so instead of the usual round or rectangular packages of filo dough, I like to shape them as Christmas crackers. For a real treat, make this recipe with the breast meat from any game bird – pigeon, dove, quail or pheasant. Allow one breast per person, or two for small birds such as quail.

1 Pour boiling water over the dried mushrooms to cover them and leave to soak. Trim the chicken breasts. Add enough stock to cover them, add the lid, bring them just to the boil and simmer for 2 minutes. Let the breasts cool in the liquid and then drain them, reserving the stock. Pull the meat into slivers. Make the *Cranberry Confit* (see opposite).

2 Make the mushroom filling: drain the dried mushrooms, rinse to remove any grit, then coarsely chop them. Next trim and coarsely chop the button mushrooms. Melt the butter in a pan and cook the shallots and garlic until fragrant, about 1 minute. Add the dried and button mushrooms and sauté until tender and all the liquid has evaporated, 5–7 minutes. Stir in the flour, cook for 1 minute and then stir in the reserved chicken stock. Bring the sauce to the boil, stirring constantly until it thickens. Simmer until it coats the back of a spoon, 2 minutes or longer if it is thin. Stir in the chicken with the Madeira and sage. Taste the filling, adjust the seasoning and let it cool.

3 To assemble the crackers: lightly brush one sheet of filo pastry with butter (don't overdo it or the package will be soggy not crisp) and put a second sheet on top. Brush with more butter, then top with a third sheet and brush again with butter. Spoon about a quarter of the mushroom filling lengthwise down the centre of the dough in a 15 x 5 cm/6 x 2 in rectangle, leaving about 5 cm/2 in at each end. Fold the pastry over the filling and roll it to form a cylinder, then twist the ends to enclose the filling and make a cracker shape. Brush with butter, then separate the ends a little to make frills. Repeat for three more crackers. Transfer them to a baking sheet, seam downwards, and chill for at least 30 minutes.

4 Heat the oven to 190°C/375°/Gas Mark 5. Slit each cracker 2–3 times to allow steam to escape, then bake until the pastry is crisp and browned and the filling is very hot, 25–30 minutes. If the frills of the crackers brown too quickly, cover them loosely with foil.

5 To serve, set a cracker on each plate, spoon some *Cranberry Confit* on the side and top with sage sprigs.

Serves 4

3 boneless, skinless chicken breasts (about 450 g/1 lb)
500 ml/16 fl oz chicken stock, more if needed
12 sheets filo pastry (about 225 g/8 oz)
110 g/4 oz melted butter
Cranberry Confit, for serving (see opposite)

For the mushroom filling

60 g/2 oz dried boletus/porcini mushrooms
250–500 ml/8–16 fl oz boiling water
110 g/4 oz button mushrooms
15 g/¹/₂ oz butter
3 shallots, finely chopped
1 garlic clove, finely chopped
2 tablespoons flour
2 tablespoons Madeira
1 tablespoon chopped sage, plus sprigs for garnish
salt and pepper

Shortcut: Make the filling with cooked chicken or even turkey at Christmas; you will need some extra chicken or turkey stock.

Getting Ahead: Prepare the crackers and sauce up to 12 hours ahead and keep them, covered, in the refrigerator. Bake the crackers as described, allowing 5 minutes longer for them to cook after chilling.

On the Side: As well as the *Cranberry Confit*, I'd consider some braised red cabbage, chestnut purée, mashed potatoes, or even all three.

In the Glass: This deserves a classic Bordeaux, whether an original from France or one of the Bordeaux-style blends coming from around the world.

CRANBERRY CONFIT
(Makes 500 ml/16 fl oz, serves 6–8)
This quick cranberry preserve adds a welcome touch of colour to the plate.

Butter a shallow ovenproof dish, then scatter 450 g/ 1 lb fresh or frozen cranberries in a single layer. Sprinkle over 200 g/7 oz sugar and stir to coat the berries. Cover the dish with foil and bake until the berries are tender, about 1 hour. If they make a lot of juice, uncover the confit for the last 15 minutes of cooking time so the liquid can evaporate. Let the confit cool, then stir so some of the berries fall apart and bind the rest together.

Lorraine Roast Goose with Apples and Swede

Goose with whole apples cooked inside is a banquet in itself, with swede and apple wedges flavoured with goose fat. Generous fat on the bird is a good sign, with white skin and plenty of plump breast meat. (The fat melts during cooking.) Dark-skinned birds with a prominent breast bone are scrawny and tough – no good to anyone. The French like their goose cooked to be pink and juicy but slightly chewy. I prefer mine very well done, almost falling off the bone with a crisp skin, and that's how I've cooked it here.

1 Heat the oven to 200°C/400°F/Gas Mark 6. Pull any loose fat from the cavity of the goose and wipe the inside with paper towels. Season inside and out with salt and pepper. Peel and core six apples, leaving them whole, and stuff them into the goose. Truss the bird with string (page 166) and put it on a rack in a roasting pan. Pour over half the beer, rubbing it well into the skin; reserve the rest.

2 Roast the goose in the oven for 15–20 minutes until the skin begins to turn brown. Reduce the oven to 180°C/350°F/Gas Mark 4 and baste thoroughly. Prick the skin all over with a fork so the melted fat can escape. Roast for about another half hour, basting often and adding more beer if the pan gets dry. A good deal of fat will accumulate in the roasting pan, so ladle it into a bowl and keep it for frying the world's best roast potatoes (see right).

3 When the breast is very brown, turn the bird breast-side down and continue roasting until the meat starts to pull from the leg bones, about another hour. If the skin browns too fast during this time, cover the goose loosely with foil. Finally turn it breast upwards and finish roasting, for a total cooking time of 2–2^1/$_2$ hours. When done, the goose will be dark brown and the legs will feel loose if you wobble the drumsticks. Pierce the thigh with a two-pronged fork – when cooked, it should feel quite tender and the juices should run clear, not pink. If you have a meat thermometer, insert it between the thigh and breast – it should read 83°C/180°F.

4 Meanwhile, cook the swede: peel them and cut into 3.5 cm/1^1/$_2$ in chunks. Put them in a pan of cold, salted water, cover and bring them to the boil. Simmer for 15–20 minutes until tender but still firm, then drain them.

5 When the goose is cooked, spread the butter over the breast. Increase the oven temperature to 230°C/450°F/Gas Mark 8 and return the bird to the oven for 5–7 minutes to crisp up the skin.

6 Meanwhile, cook the remaining apples: peel the apples, cut them into wedges, and sprinkle with the sugar. Heat 2 tablespoons of the reserved goose fat in a large frying pan and fry the apples quickly over a high heat to brown them, 2–3 minutes. Set them aside and keep warm.

7 Add a little more of the fat to the pan, add the swede with salt and pepper and fry rapidly until very hot and starting to brown, stirring occasionally, 3–5 minutes. Keep them warm also.

8 Transfer the bird to a serving platter, discarding the strings, and keep warm. To make the gravy: pour off the fat from the pan, leaving about a tablespoon with the pan juices. Stir in the flour and cook on top of the stove until browned, 1–2 minutes. Stir in the stock and remaining beer and bring to the boil, stirring to dissolve the pan juices. Simmer until slightly thickened, 3–5 minutes. Strain it into a small pan, bring to the boil and season it to taste.

9 To serve: spoon the swede and apples around the goose, or serve in separate dishes, not forgetting the tender, well flavoured apples inside the bird. Decorate the platter with herbs and serve the gravy in a separate bowl.

Serves 6–8

4–4.5 kg/9–10 lb goose, cleaned and oven ready

salt and pepper

8 tart apples (about 1.35 kg/3 lb), such as Granny Smith

300 ml/10 fl oz dark beer, more if needed

675 g/1^1/$_2$ lb swede

30 g/1 oz butter

1 tablespoon sugar

1 tablespoon flour

500 ml/16 fl oz chicken stock

fresh herbs and greens such as sage and lamb's lettuce, to garnish

Getting Ahead: Let's face it, a festive bird always needs attention as it cooks, so you might as well look after the accompaniments at the same time so they are freshly cooked and at their best.

On the Side: Born in England, I go for Brussels sprouts and potatoes roasted in goose fat, the world's best.

In the Glass: A great dish deserves a great wine. The province of Lorraine was once part of the dukedom of Burgundy, so what better partner could there be for this sumptuous goose than a fine Burgundy or Pinot Noir?

POTATOES ROASTED WITH GOOSE FAT
(Serves 8)
Cut 1.35 kg/3 lb potatoes into large chunks and parboil them. Drain and dry well. At least an hour before the goose is cooked, heat 3–4 tablespoons of the reserved goose fat in a roasting pan in the oven. When very hot, put in the potatoes and turn in the fat. Cook in the oven, on a shelf above the goose, until crisp, golden and very tender, about 1 hour. Sprinkle the potatoes with salt just before serving.

Roast Pigeon with Thyme, Raspberries and Whisky Gravy

Serves 4

8 thyme sprigs

4 tablespoons Scotch whisky

330 g/12 oz raspberries

4 pigeons, cleaned and oven ready

30 g/1 oz butter

salt and pepper

8 streaky bacon slices

1 tablespoon flour

250 ml/8 fl oz chicken stock

1 tablespoon redcurrant jelly

Inspiration for this recipe comes from Scotland, a country famous for its raspberries, and above all its grouse, game birds that can fly at nearly 100 km/60 miles an hour. Grouse are dark-fleshed and pungent but only seasonally available; cook them in just the same way as the pigeon that is the nearest readily available alternative.

1 Heat the oven to 220°C/425°F/Gas Mark 7. Set aside four sprigs of thyme for decoration. Pound the rest in a mortar and pestle, or with a heavy pan. Pour over 3 tablespoons of whisky and leave to soak.

2 Crush half of the raspberries and put them inside the pigeons. Spread the birds with butter, sprinkle with salt and pepper and lay the soaked thyme on top. Wrap the birds with sliced bacon so they are held firmly and set them in a roasting pan. Pour over any whisky left from the thyme. Roast the birds, turning occasionally, for 30 minutes, until well browned and legs do not resist when pulled.

3 Transfer the pigeons to a dish, cover with foil and keep them warm. To make the sauce: discard all but a tablespoon of fat from the pan. Stir in the flour and cook until brown, 1–2 minutes. Pour in the chicken stock and bring to the boil, stirring to dissolve the pan juices. Simmer until reduced and slightly thickened, 2–3 minutes. Strain the sauce into a small pan, whisk in the jelly and stir over a low heat until melted. Then stir in the remaining raspberries and a tablespoon of whisky and cook for 1 minute until the raspberries are just soft. Season the sauce to taste.

4 Discard the strings from the pigeons and set them on warm individual plates or a platter. Spoon over a little sauce and decorate with sprigs of thyme.

On the Side: You must try *Stovies* (page 69), a potato dish that is universally popular in Scotland.

In the Glass: A forthright red from the Rhône, or a clone based on the Syrah grape.

Californian Pot-roast of Veal with Dried Fruit

The farmers' markets of California are a cornucopia of dried as well as fresh fruits. It was here that I learned that the best dried fruits look beige and a bit tired – bright colours are not to be trusted, usually a sign of the use of sulphur as a preservative. For pot-roasting, I like veal to be firmly tied so it carves into neat slices for serving; in the US I look for rump or sirloin, and in the UK for rump or fillet. As a more economical dish for the family, I make this recipe with pork loin.

Serves 6–8

250 ml/8 fl oz apple juice

200 g/7 oz dried prunes

200 g/7 oz dried apricots

75 g/2¹/₂ oz flour

salt and pepper

1.5 kg/3¹/₂–4 lb boneless veal roast, tied with string

2 tablespoons vegetable oil

2 onions, sliced

1 tablespoon brown sugar

¹/₂ teaspoon ground cinnamon

¹/₂ teaspoon ground ginger

3 whole cloves

250 ml/8 fl oz dry white wine

500 ml/16 fl oz veal or chicken stock

1 Heat the oven to 160°C/325°F/Gas Mark 3. Bring the apple juice to the boil, pour it over the prunes and apricots and leave to soak. Then season the flour generously with salt and pepper on a plate and roll the veal in it until coated.

2 Heat the oil in a casserole and brown the meat thoroughly on all sides. Stir the onion into the pot, with the sugar, cinnamon, ginger and cloves. Add the wine and simmer for 2 minutes. Pour in the stock, cover the pot and bring to the boil on top of the stove. Cook the veal in the oven for 1 hour, basting and turning it occasionally. If it gets dry, add a cup of water.

3 After an hour, stir the fruit with any juice into the pot, with enough water to cover the fruit if needed. Continue cooking and basting until the meat is very tender when pierced with a two-pronged fork, ¹/₂–1 hour longer.

4 Transfer the veal to a carving board and cover it with foil to keep warm. Taste the gravy and adjust the seasoning – it should be concentrated with a lively flavour. If thin, boil it on top of the stove to reduce it. Slice the pot-roast and arrange it on a platter with the fruits and a little gravy. Serve the remaining gravy separately, discarding the whole cloves.

Shortcut: To shorten cooking time, substitute 6–8 veal medallions for the whole roast. Brown the medallions, add the onion, sugar, spices, wine and stock. Bring to the boil and at once add the fruit. Continue cooking as directed.

Getting Ahead: Pot-roast improves if you cook it ahead. It keeps well in the refrigerator for at least three days. Reheat it with the fruits and gravy on top of the stove, then slice it just before serving.

On the Side: In the old days, pot-roast would always be served with mashed potatoes to absorb the lovely gravy, but fresh fettuccine would be an alternative, now that it is so readily available.

In the Glass: Red wine for me, a hearty Zinfandel, or a Shiraz.

Roast Pork with a Herb-mustard Crust

Rack of pork – the loin including the rib bones – makes an excellent party roast when topped with a savoury breadcrumb mixture that cooks to be brown and crisp. The topping sticks to the meat surface, thanks to a brushing with Dijon mustard, which can be mild or hot, according to your taste. Dijon, or any French mustard, is perfect for cooking as the flavour is so complex. Take your pick of mustard from Dijon, which has a clean, sharp taste, smooth and mild Bordeaux mustard, or mustard from Meaux, which is dark and rougher in texture as it includes seeds. The pork is just as delicious served cold as it is hot.

Serves 6–8

1.5 kg/3–4 lb pork loin, with rib bones
salt and pepper
2 tablespoons vegetable oil

For the topping
45 g/1¹⁄₂ oz butter
2–3 garlic cloves, chopped
2 shallots, chopped
1 teaspoon ground cumin
1 teaspoon ground paprika
5–6 tablespoons chopped parsley
90 g/3 oz dry browned breadcrumbs
3 tablespoons Dijon mustard

For the gravy
250 ml/8 fl oz medium dry white wine
375 ml/12 fl oz veal or chicken stock

1 Heat the oven to 200°C/400°F/Gas Mark 6. Trim any excess fat from the pork. If necessary, scrape the rib bones clean. Sprinkle the meat with salt and pepper. Heat the oil in a roasting pan and brown the fat-covered surface of the pork over medium heat, taking 5–7 minutes. Set the roast ribs-down and roast it in the oven, basting occasionally, 30 minutes.

2 Meanwhile, make the topping: melt the butter and sauté the garlic and shallots until soft and fragrant, 2–3 minutes. Stir in the cumin and paprika and continue cooking 1 minute. Take from the heat and stir in the parsley and breadcrumbs.

3 After 30 minutes' cooking, brush the surface of the pork with the mustard and spread it with the topping, pressing so it forms a crust. Turn down the oven heat to 190°C/375°F/Gas Mark 5. Continue roasting the meat without basting for another 30–40 minutes, until a skewer inserted in the centre of the meat is hot to the touch when withdrawn. A meat thermometer should register 72°C/165°F. Transfer the meat to a platter and cover it loosely with foil.

4 For the gravy: add the wine to the roasting pan and simmer, stirring to dissolve pan juices, until the wine is reduced almost to a glaze. Add the stock and simmer until well flavoured, 2 minutes or longer if necessary. Strain the gravy into a small pan, reheat it and taste for seasoning. For serving, carve the pork at table, cutting vertically down between the rib bones to form chops. Serve the gravy separately.

Getting Ahead: By all means prepare the pork and topping ahead, but the meat must be freshly roasted if you are serving it hot.

On the Side: My favourite accompaniment for almost any roast meat is potatoes, pan-roasted in the oven with the meat and perfect with the pan gravy. You'll find out all about it and other potato ideas on page 69. If you prefer to serve the pork cold, I would add a salad of root vegetables such as beetroot, celery or simply potatoes, dressed in an olive oil and balsamic vinaigrette.

In the Glass: To partner mustard from Dijon, a Pinot Noir would be in order, perhaps from Oregon, South Africa or Chile instead of Burgundy itself.

Braised Leg of Lamb with Juniper

Braised Leg of Lamb with Juniper – *or* Gigot d'Agneau des Garrigues – *comes from the south-sloping mountains of Languedoc, to the west of Provence, which are carpeted with wild herbs that flourish in the Mediterranean sun. Thyme, bay and juniper are among the most aromatic, here bolstered by a shot of gin (juniper berries provide the lead flavour in gin). To intensify the flavour, I like to spike the lamb with garlic and juniper berries up to 24 hours ahead, and then braise it slowly in the style of the famous French recipe for seven-hour leg of lamb. It becomes deliciously moist and tender, almost falling from the bone.*

1 Trim the skin and all but a thin layer of fat from the lamb. With the point of a knife, make 8–10 incisions in the meaty part of the lamb and insert some of the garlic and a few crushed juniper berries in each. Cover with clingfilm and chill for 24 hours so the flavours permeate the meat. Reserve the remaining garlic and juniper berries.

2 Preheat the oven to 180°C/350°F/Gas Mark 4. Unwrap the lamb and season it with salt and pepper. Heat the oil in a roasting pan or casserole, then brown the lamb on all sides over medium heat until well browned, 7–10 minutes. Take it out, add the onions and brown them also, taking 5–7 minutes and stirring often so they don't scorch. Replace the lamb in the pan, and add the gin, stock and reserved garlic and juniper berries. Tie the thyme and bay leaves in two or three bundles and add to the casserole. Bring to the boil and cover tightly with a lid or foil.

3 Braise the lamb in the oven, turning it once or twice, until the meat is very tender when pierced with a fork. This will take 2–2¹/₂ hours, or up to an hour longer if you like the meat almost falling off the bone. The meat should always be half-covered in liquid, so add more stock during cooking if needed.

4 Meanwhile, wipe the fresh mushrooms, trimming the stems; wash them only if they are dirty. Slice them, or cut them into medium chunks. If using dried mushrooms, cover them with warm water and leave them to soak.

5 Half an hour before the lamb is done, stir the mushrooms and pepper into the cooking juices. If using dried mushrooms, lift them out of the water with a draining spoon, leaving any grit behind; add them to the pan.

6 When done, transfer the lamb to a serving dish. Remove the mushrooms, pepper and onions with a draining spoon and pile around the lamb; cover and keep warm. Strain the cooking juices into a pan and skim any fat from the surface. Bring this gravy to the boil and, if thin, boil until reduced. Taste and adjust the seasoning. Spoon a little gravy over the meat and scatter parsley over the vegetables. Serve the remaining gravy separately.

Shortcut: Don't bother to marinate the meat in advance with garlic and juniper, but braise it straight away.

Getting Ahead: Braised lamb reheats superbly, taking on extra depth of flavour as it sits, up to three days in the refrigerator. To reheat it, wrap the lamb leg in foil and heat it in a 200°C/400°F/Gas Mark 6 oven until very hot, 20–30 minutes. Reheat the vegetables and gravy separately on top of the stove.

On the Side: One of the half dozen ideas from 'Potatoes for All' (page 69), plus *Roasted Butternut Squash* (see right).

In the Glass: Languedoc makes some excellent, inexpensive red wines, or you could move over the border for a Spanish Rioja.

Serves 6–8

1 leg of lamb on the bone (about 2.25 kg/5 lb)

4 garlic cloves, cut into slivers

1 tablespoon juniper berries, crushed

salt and pepper

3 tablespoons olive oil

3 onions, sliced

125 ml/4 fl oz gin

575 ml/1 pint chicken stock, more if needed

bunch of fresh thyme

2–3 bay leaves

450 g/1 lb wild or cultivated mushrooms, or
  60 g/2 oz dried wild mushrooms

1 red pepper, seeded and cut into strips

chopped fresh parsley, to garnish

ROASTED BUTTERNUT SQUASH
(Serves 4)
When butternut squash is thinly sliced and roasted on a baking sheet, the skin toasts to be deliciously tender. Serve the squash with meats and game in autumn.

Heat the oven to 190°C/375°F/Gas Mark 5. With a large chef's knife, cut a medium butternut squash (about 1.35 kg/3 lb) in half lengthwise and scoop out the seeds. Set each half flat on a cutting board and cut crosswise in 1 cm/³/₈ in slices. Melt 30–45 g/1–1¹/₂ oz butter with 2–3 tablespoons olive oil and generously brush a heavy baking sheet. Line up the squash slices on the baking sheet and brush them also. Sprinkle with 1 teaspoon sugar, salt and pepper. Between and under the slices tuck 6–8 sprigs each of thyme and rosemary, and 3–4 bay leaves. Cover with foil and bake in the oven for 30 minutes. Remove the foil and continue baking until the undersides are brown, about 15 minutes, then turn the slices. Bake for 5–15 minutes more until the squash is very tender, brown and crispy around the edges, 50–60 minutes total. Don't hesitate to brush with more butter and oil during cooking if it looks dry.

Venison and Mushroom Pie with Port

My mother's game pie was famous – her secret? Adding a spoonful of chopped pickled walnuts to give the sauce depth and colour. The same amount of black oil-cured olives, chopped, will give similar colour.

Serves 6

450 g/1 lb boneless venison

450 g/1 lb chuck steak

175 ml/6 fl oz port

4 shallots, finely chopped

1 tablespoon pickled walnuts, finely chopped

3 tablespoons flour

salt and pepper

750 ml/1¼ pints brown or veal stock (page 166), more if needed

450 g/1 lb portabella or large flat mushrooms, cut into wedges

450 g/1 lb puff pastry dough

1 egg, beaten and mixed with ½ teaspoon salt, for glaze

1.75-litre/3-pint pie dish

1 To make the filling: cut the venison and steak in 4 cm/1½ in pieces, trimming any sinew. Put them in a heavy plastic bag and add the port. Seal the bag and leave the meat to marinate in a bowl in the refrigerator for 1–2 days.

2 Heat the oven to 180°C/350°F/Gas Mark 4. In a large bowl, mix together the shallots, pickled walnuts and flour with a teaspoon each of salt and pepper. Lift the meat from the port with a draining spoon, reserving the marinade, and stir the meat into the flour, so it gets coated thoroughly. Transfer this mixture to a large ovenproof casserole. Stir together the reserved marinade and stock, then stir the liquid into the casserole along with the mushrooms. Bring it to the boil over medium heat, stirring occasionally until the sauce thickens lightly. Cover and cook the casserole in the oven until the meat is almost tender when pierced with a fork, 1½–2 hours. The meat should always be covered with sauce, so add more stock during cooking if needed.

3 Remove the lid and simmer the casserole on top of the stove until the sauce is quite thick, stirring often, 15–20 minutes. Taste, adjust the seasoning and spoon the mixture into the pie dish. Leave it to cool thoroughly.

4 To assemble the pie: roll the pastry dough to an oval 2.5 cm/1 in larger than the pie dish. Trim the edges and cut a strip the width of the dish rim from the edge of the dough. Brush the rim of the dish with water and lay the strip of dough on the rim, pressing down so it sticks. Brush the dough strip with the egg glaze.

5 Wrap the dough oval around the rolling pin and lift it on to the pie dish. Press the dough firmly to seal it to the strip. Trim excess dough and brush the top of the pie with egg glaze. Make two small slits in the centre of the dough to allow steam to escape. Roll out any trimmings and use them to cut out flowers or leaves to decorate the pie. Brush the decorations with egg glaze. Chill the pie for at least 15 minutes before baking.

6 Heat the oven to 220°C/425°F/Gas Mark 7 and bake the pie until the pastry is puffed, crisp and golden, 25–35 minutes.

Getting Ahead: This is an ideal make-ahead dish. Cook the venison filling and chill it thoroughly in the pie dish. Top with the dough and pastry decorations, chill until the dough is very firm, and then wrap the pie carefully to chill for up to two days, or freeze for three months. Thaw the pie if necessary and bake it as directed.

On the Side: With venison pie, at home in rural England we had root vegetables – mashed potatoes, mashed swede, boiled carrots – and cabbage. Now I might take quite a different route, with *Roasted Butternut Squash* (page 125).

In the Glass: The traditional accompaniment to a fine game dish is a top French red wine, either a Burgundy, or an Hermitage or Côte-Rôtie from the Rhône Valley. For this special recipe, they are worth the outlay.

We all have our favourite recipes, the rewarding little dishes that can be run up in a hurry from ingredients that are easy to find. Here are mine.

Melon and Tomato Salad (Serves 4)

I always think melon is best when served as simply as possible – this recipe has only three other ingredients.

Peel 225 g/8 oz cherry tomatoes (page 166). Halve a large melon and discard the seeds. Next scoop out the flesh in balls with a melon-ball cutter and add to the tomatoes. Scrape and discard leftover flesh from the melon shells and halve them to form four crescents. Strip the leaves from a bunch of basil, reserving four sprigs for garnish. Finely shred the leaves and add to the fruit. Stir 125 ml/4 fl oz sweet vermouth or port into the fruit, with salt, pepper and a pinch of sugar if you feel it is needed. Taste and adjust the seasoning. Cover and refrigerate the fruit, with the melon shells separately, for at least 1 hour and up to 8 hours. To serve: set the melon shells on plates and pile the fruit in the shells, spooning over the juice. Top with a basil sprig.

Orange Salad with Olives (Serves 4)

Try it as an appetizer, as an accompaniment to duck or pork, or as an offbeat dessert. If you use blood oranges, the visual effect with the dark olives is spectacular.

Pare the zest from 2 large navel oranges and cut it in very fine julienne strips. Cut the peel, pith and skin from these and 2 more oranges, to make 4 in all. Cut the oranges in 1 cm/3/8 in slices (reserve any juice) and pile them in a glass bowl, or in individual bowls, layering them with 40 g/11/2 oz oil-cured black olives, pitted and coarsely chopped. Put 175 ml/6 fl oz orange juice in a saucepan with any juice from the oranges and add 60 g/2 oz brown sugar and 1/4 teaspoon each of ground cloves and nutmeg. Bring slowly to the boil, stirring until the sugar dissolves, then simmer 5 minutes. Let cool to tepid and pour over the oranges.

To caramelize the orange julienne: put them in a small pan with 3 tablespoons sugar and 3 tablespoons water. Heat gently until the sugar dissolves, then cook until the liquid evaporates and the julienne are tender and translucent, 8 to 10 minutes. Scatter them over the oranges. Cover and chill for at least 3 and up to 24 hours. Just before serving, taste the syrup. If very tart, sprinkle it with more sugar. Serve chilled.

Hot and Sweet Red Pepper Dip (Serves 4–6)

This Lebanese dip is delicious served with pitta bread, or as a sauce for barbecued chicken or fish.

Light a grill or barbecue and oil the rack. Set 450 g/ 1 lb red peppers and 1–2 chilli peppers on the rack and roast them, turning them often until they are blackened and blistered all over, 8–12 minutes. Drop them in a plastic bag, seal it and leave to cool so the steam loosens the skins. Peel off the skins. Halve the peppers and chillies and remove the stems, ribs and seeds. Spread them, skinned-side up, on paper towels and leave them to drain. (If the chillies are too small to peel, don't worry, simply core and seed them.)

Put 100 g/31/2 oz walnut pieces, 3 tablespoons dry breadcrumbs, 1 tablespoon redcurrant jelly, 1 table- spoon red wine vinegar, 2 tablespoons lemon juice, 1/2 teaspoon cumin and 1/2 teaspoon salt in the bowl of a food processor. Purée until smooth. Add the peppers with half the chillies and process until puréed and creamy. With the machine on, add 1 tablespoon of olive oil in a thin stream. Taste and adjust the seasoning, adding more chilli, vinegar or lemon juice to taste. If it is too thick, thin it with 1–2 tablespoons water. For serving, spread it in a bowl and drizzle with olive oil.

Corn Cakes (Makes about 12)

Serve these full size as an appetizer with smoked salmon or prosciutto, and sour cream. Made cocktail size, they become canapés when topped with herbed goats' cheese or cream cheese sprinkled with chives.

In a bowl, mix 200 g/7 oz yellow cornmeal, 30 g/1 oz flour, a pinch of baking soda and a large pinch of salt. Crumble 2 tablespoons cream cheese in another bowl and beat in 1 egg and 3 tablespoons buttermilk. Stir this into the flour, then add 4 tablespoons fresh or cooked corn kernels. The batter will be quite stiff. Heat 1–2 tablespoons oil in a large frying pan and drop spoonfuls of batter, flattening them with the back of a wet spoon to form 5 cm/2 in rounds. Fry for 2–3 minutes until golden, turn and fry the other side. Transfer the cakes to a plate, piling them one on another to keep warm, while frying the rest.

TIPS FOR DIPPING

Herbed Olives: Give a bowl of olives a personal touch. Heat 250 ml/8 fl oz olive oil with 2 sprigs thyme, 2 sprigs rosemary, 2 bay leaves, 2 finely chopped garlic cloves, freshly ground pepper and a pinch of red pepper flakes. When the oil just simmers remove from the heat, stir, and leave it to cool to room temperature. Adjust the seasoning as you like. Put 675g/11/2 lb green olives in a jar and pour the oil over them. Allow to cool completely, then cover and keep in a cool place for up to a week. For serving, drain the olives and serve at room temperature. The oil is great for grilling.
Curried Nuts: You can't make enough of these. Melt 30 g/1 oz butter in a pan. Stir in 1 teaspoon paprika, 1 teaspoon curry powder and 1/2 teaspoon salt. Heat gently, stirring, until the spices are fragrant and toasted. Put 225 g/8 oz walnuts or pecans in a bowl and pour the butter over them, tossing to coat. Spread them on a buttered baking sheet and toast in a 180°C/350°F/Gas Mark 4 oven for 8–12 minutes, until crisp. Serve warm or at room temperature.

I often turn to fruit for inspiration when I'm searching for quick dessert ideas. So much so that this chapter is almost exclusively devoted to cooking with fruit. Cherries, for instance, take less than 5 minutes to simmer in red wine if you don't bother to remove the stones, and the batter for an apple or pear pudding is equally quick to mix. Just last week we had unexpected visitors, an invitation to flambé ripe plums and peaches from the garden (it's August, with the best fruit crop I can remember).

The seasons are important when cooking with fruit. Forget that strawberries are available in markets all year round – when freshly picked from a local patch, their summer fragrance transforms the simplest recipe. In winter, warming dishes such as flambéed bananas and stuffed baked apples (try my combination of muesli and honey) come into their own. A whole fresh pineapple roasted with spikes of vanilla bean is a gourmet treat that will perfume your kitchen on a dark day.

A stock of ice cream in the freezer can be a boon for quick desserts (don't store it too long as ice cream, and particularly sorbet, will crystallize). Ice cream is the ideal companion to many fruit desserts, and to the rapidly mixed *Almond and Cape Gooseberry Torte* and *California Cornmeal Cake* that you'll find in this chapter. If you whisk up a quick home-made sauce, ice cream is fine on its own. And I have a couple of ideas for personalizing commercial ice cream by letting it soften, then stirring in crushed ginger cookies, or a combination of nuts and candied fruit. You'll be surprised by the delicious results.

Fast Finishes

Vanilla Roasted Pineapple

A whole pineapple spiked with sticks of vanilla pod, then roasted until it is caramelized, will fill your kitchen with fragrance. If you come across little individual pineapples, allow one per person – a treat indeed!

1 Heat the oven to 160°C/325°F/Gas Mark 3. Cut the plume and base from the pineapple and set it upright. Following the curve of the fruit, cut away the skin and hollow out the eyes with the point of a knife. Cut out the core with an apple corer. Spear the fruit with pieces of vanilla. Stand the pineapple upright in a baking dish.

2 Heat the sugar, water, ginger, orange and lemon zest and juice in a small pan, stirring gently until the sugar dissolves. Pour the syrup over the pineapple and roast it in the oven, basting often until the pineapple browns and the syrup starts to caramelize, $1^1/4$–$1^1/2$ hours. Toward the end of cooking, keep a close watch as the syrup will scorch rapidly once it cooks to a glaze.

3 Slice the pineapple into thick rings and serve warm, basted with the cooking syrup and topped with a scoop of ice cream. I often leave the pieces of vanilla for decoration, though I'm afraid you cannot eat them. (If you like you can wash them after use, dry them and store in the sugar jar to make vanilla sugar.)

Serves 4–6

1 large ripe pineapple
4 vanilla pods, each cut into 2–3 sticks
110 g/4 oz light brown sugar
125 ml/4 fl oz water
about 1 tablespoon grated fresh ginger
grated zest and juice of 1 orange
grated zest and juice of 1 lemon

Shortcut: Buy a whole pineapple that has already been peeled and cored.

Getting Ahead: Roast the pineapple ahead and store it for up to three days in the refrigerator. It is delicious at room temperature, or warm it gently in the oven.

On the Side: I like to serve it with coconut ice cream or any nut ice cream.

In the Glass: Perhaps a fruity Sauvignon Blanc – the citrus notes will complement the pineapple's glaze.

Cherries Chateaux

Very occasionally, a recipe defies the rules and this is one. The name Chateaux *has nothing to do with a French castle, but comes from the Romanian word,* satou, *a version of the fluffy sauce better known as sabayon. Sabayon is delicious but impractical as it has to be whisked at the last minute because it separates so easily.* Chateaux, *however, keeps for hours and never separates. I like to use a white wine with a bit of body for this recipe, such as a Chardonnay or Riesling.*

Makes 1 litre/1³/₄ pints, to serve 6–8

8 egg yolks
150 g/5¹/₂ oz sugar
finely grated zest of 1 small orange or 1 lemon
500 ml/16 fl oz medium-dry white wine
450 g/1 lb cherries, stoned

electric hand-mixer

1 Beat the egg yolks, sugar and orange or lemon zest in an electric hand-mixer at high speed for 7–8 minutes until pale and very thick – this will also help to develop the citrus flavour. Meanwhile, bring the wine just to the boil in a heavy-based pan.
2 With the mixer on low speed, add the hot wine to the egg-yolk mixture. Return the custard to the pan and cook it over low heat, stirring constantly with a wooden spoon, until it thickens and lightly coats the back of the spoon, 3–4 minutes. A clear trail should be left in the custard on the spoon when you draw your finger over it. Do not let it boil; if it gets too hot or cooks for too long, it may curdle.
3 Pour the custard into a cold bowl set over ice and allow to cool, stirring occasionally. Serve at room temperature or chilled, poured over the cherries.

Getting Ahead: *Chateaux* can be made several hours in advance and kept covered in the refrigerator. If it separates slightly, simply whisk it to remix just before serving.

On the Side: Think of *Chateaux* as adult egg custard. It marries happily with many things, including cake, berries and poached fruit as well as the cherries I suggest here.

In the Glass: A delicate custard like this cries out for a fine sweet wine such as a late-picked Riesling, or a French Sauternes if your budget allows.

Chocolate Cherries

Chocolate cherries can't be kept for more than a day, but they're so tempting there's little chance they will last that long!

Coats 20–25 cherries

225 g/8 oz large cherries with stems
225 g/8 oz good-quality dark, white or milk
  chocolate, chopped
1 tablespoon vegetable oil

1 Discard any damaged cherries. Thoroughly wash and dry the rest. Put the chocolate in a small, deep saucepan or bowl over a pan of hot but not boiling water or use a double-boiler. Heat the chocolate until melted, stirring occasionally. Take it from the heat, stir in the oil and let cool to tepid.
2 Have ready a sheet of non-stick baking paper. Dip a cherry in the melted chocolate, let excess drain into the pan for a few seconds, then set the cherry on the paper. If the chocolate forms a 'foot' on the paper it's too warm, so let it cool a bit more and try again. Coat the rest of the cherries. If the chocolate in the pan starts to set, gently heat the pan in warm water.
3 Chill the cherries until set, then peel them off the paper. They will have lost their gloss, but will regain it if they are left at room temperature.

Getting Ahead: Keep the cherries for up to 24 hours in a cool place or in the refrigerator.

On the Side: Serve *Chocolate Cherries* with coffee after dinner, or use them to decorate cakes and desserts.

In the Glass: A shot of cherry brandy.

Volcanic Apples

These apples are hollowed to the shape of a volcano so they take more stuffing, hence their name in our family. For the filling, I'm calling for muesli as it is so easy to find, but you'll save a bit of time if you use granola, which is already toasted. Simply mix it with the other ingredients. You'll need a tart variety of apple that will be fluffy and juicy when baked; traditional favourites are Cox's or Reine de Reinettes, though you can always fall back on the ubiquitous Granny Smith.

Serves 4

4 medium apples (about 675 g/1¹/₂ lb)

45 g/1¹/₂ oz butter

75 g/2¹/₂ oz muesli, preferably containing dried fruit and nuts

40 g/1¹/₂ oz walnuts, coarsely chopped

60 g/2 oz brown sugar

¹/₂ teaspoon ground cinnamon

4 tablespoons honey

1 Heat the oven to 190°C/375°F/Gas Mark 5. Wash and core the apples, scooping out a hollow in the top to hold the filling. Slash the skin of each apple horizontally around its equator so the flesh can expand without bursting the skin.
2 Melt the butter in a non-stick frying pan and add the muesli, walnuts and brown sugar. Toast for 3–5 minutes, stirring constantly, until the muesli starts to brown. Remove from the heat and stir in the cinnamon. Set the apples in a shallow baking dish; they should not quite touch each other in the dish so heat can circulate. Push some of the mixture into the hollow of each apple, mounding it on top, and pour a spoonful of honey over each one. Add a few tablespoons of water to the dish.
3 Bake the apples, basting occasionally so the honey forms a glaze, until they are tender when pierced with a skewer, 40–50 minutes. Towards the end of cooking, keep an eye on the dish and add a little water if the honey shows signs of scorching.
4 Serve the apples hot, with the honey syrup spooned over as a sauce.

Getting Ahead: Baked apples are pretty good cooked ahead, then reheated gently in the oven. They will keep in the refrigerator for up to two days.

On the Side: Ice cream, yoghurt or a pitcher of the richest double cream you can find.

In the Glass: Let's have more apple, with a mug of cider.

Herbed Strawberry Fool with Yoghurt

We grow a great variety of herbs at home in Burgundy, and this recipe suits many of the more unusual ones such as lemon balm, lemon thyme, sweet geranium and woodruff; mint would be a more conventional choice. 'Fool', a teasing title for a puréed dessert, sounds like a culinary insult but is, I'm convinced, derived from the French fouler, to press or sieve – precisely what it takes to make this dessert. Other tart fruits are also good, such as raspberries and poached rhubarb.

1 Chill the cream, bowl and whisk in the freezer for about 5–10 minutes before starting. (To save washing up the mixer, I whisk this small amount of cream by hand.) The cream and glasses for serving should also be chilled in the refrigerator. Put the cream in the chilled bowl and whisk until it holds a soft peak when the whisk is lifted.

2 Reserve four herb sprigs for decoration. Chop the remaining leaves, discarding the stems. Hull the strawberries and purée two-thirds in the food processor or blender. Stir in the kirsch or lemon juice and sugar to taste. Slice the remaining berries, reserving two of the best for topping, and stir in the chopped herb.

3 Add the purée to the cream and fold the two together lightly but thoroughly to make the fool. As you fold, the cream will thicken a little because of the acid in the purée. Stir in the yoghurt.

4 To assemble the dessert, spoon the fool into the chilled glasses, filling them about one-third full. Sprinkle with the sliced berries. Add more fool, then a second layer of berries. Fill with the remaining fool and top each glass with a herb sprig and half a whole berry.

Getting Ahead: *Herbed Strawberry Fool* rests happily in the refrigerator for up to a day and the flavours mellow. It will thicken on standing and a bit of pink berry syrup may pool in the bottom of the glass. Add the decoration of strawberry and herb sprig just before serving.

On the Side: Try a 'Small Diversion' (page 164).

In the Glass: A bit of fizz, with a sparkling white wine that is sweet or dry, to your taste.

Serves 4

125 ml/4 fl oz double cream
small bunch of chosen herb (about 30 g/1 oz)
225 g/8 oz strawberries
2 tablespoons kirsch or lemon juice
60 g/2 oz sugar, or more to taste
125 ml/4 fl oz natural yoghurt

4 large stemmed glasses
food processor or blender

French Pear Batter Pudding

You'll find this batter pudding throughout France under names such as clafoutis *and* flognarde *adapted to local fruit alcohols and fruits including cherries, apples, plums and prunes (in the winter). Flognarde comes from the Auvergne and can be made with pears or apples.*

1 Heat the oven to 190°C/375°F/Gas Mark 5. Butter the baking dish, sprinkle it with sugar and turn the dish so it is evenly coated, discarding excess sugar. Peel, core and slice the pears in crescents. Sprinkle the slices with the lemon juice so they don't discolour and spread in the baking dish.
2 Make the batter: put the sugar in a bowl, add the eggs and whisk for 1–2 minutes until light and frothy. Stir in the flour and salt just until smooth. Don't beat the batter at this stage as this will make the pudding tough. Stir in the milk, and strain the batter over the pears to remove any lumps of flour.
3 Bake the pudding for 55–65 minutes until it is puffed and brown. It should be firm in the centre and will have started to pull away from the sides of the dish. Let it cool for 5–10 minutes, then sprinkle with the alcohol. (The aroma from the hot alcohol is a treat in itself.) Dust it generously with the icing sugar and serve warm.

Serves 6

3–4 large ripe pears (about 675 g/1½ lb)
butter and sugar for the baking dish
juice of 1 lemon

For the batter
60 g/2 oz sugar
4 eggs
30 g/1 oz unbleached plain white flour
pinch of salt
250 ml/8 fl oz milk
3 tablespoons pear or other fruit alcohol, or rum
icing sugar for sprinkling

1.5-litre/2½-pint baking dish

On the Side: In France a bowl of crème fraîche would be my first thought, but vanilla ice cream is pretty good, too.

In the Glass: A tot of that same fruit alcohol.

Almond and Cape Gooseberry Torte

As the title implies, I first came across this recipe in South Africa, where Cape gooseberries grow in abundance. Since then the torte has become a family institution, made with raspberries, gooseberries, plums, apples or any tart fruit in season.

1 Heat the oven to 180°C/350°F/Gas Mark 4. Butter the tin, line the base with non-stick baking paper, butter and flour it. Hull the Cape gooseberries, setting aside six for decoration. Sift together the flour, baking powder, cinnamon and salt. In the mixer, cream the butter, add the sugar and beat until soft and light. Beat in the egg. Stir in the almonds and flour. The batter will be quite stiff.

2 Spread half the batter in the prepared cake tin. Sprinkle the Cape gooseberries on top and dot with remaining cake mixture so the fruit is almost covered. Bake in the oven for 45–50 minutes until the cake starts to shrink from the sides of the tin and the top is firm when lightly pressed with a fingertip. When baked, the top will be rough like a crumble, with glimpses of fruit in between.

3 Let the cake cool 10–15 minutes in the tin, then unmould it on to a rack. Set a serving plate on top, turn the cake top upwards on to the plate and leave it to cool. Sprinkle it with icing sugar and serve it warm or at room temperature.

Getting Ahead: *Almond and Cape Gooseberry Torte* keeps well in an airtight container for up to a week and simply gets more moist and delicious.

On the Side: I'd suggest natural yoghurt folded into an equal quantity of whipped cream.

In the Glass: This torte can be an all-day event, with a glass of milk at breakfast, a cup of coffee at noon, tea in the afternoon, or a sweet white wine at dinner.

Serves 6

225 g/8 oz Cape gooseberries

125 g/4^1/2 oz unbleached plain white flour, more for the pan

1^1/2 teaspoons baking powder

1 teaspoon ground cinnamon

^{1}/2 teaspoon salt

140 g/5 oz butter, more for the pan

150 g/5^1/2 oz sugar

1 egg

140 g/5 oz ground almonds

icing sugar (for sprinkling)

20 cm/8 in cake tin

electric mixer

California Cornmeal Cake

This food-processor cake has everything – earthy flavour, rich golden colour, and an unexpected crunch on the tongue. With its generous flavouring of Chardonnay wine, I think of it as typically Californian. For a non-alcoholic version simply substitute apple juice. Ice cream flavoured with roast bananas (see below) is a perfect accompaniment.

1 Heat the oven to 180°C/350°F/Gas Mark 4. Butter the cake tin, line the base with non-stick baking paper, butter the paper and coat the tin with flour.
2 Next put the flour, baking powder and salt into the food processor. Add the cornmeal or polenta, almonds, butter and sugar. Work the mixture, using the pulse button, until it forms fine crumbs, about 30 seconds.
3 With the blades turning, add the eggs and wine and pulse until smooth. Pour the batter into the cake tin and bake until the cake starts to shrink from the sides of the tin and springs back when lightly pressed with a fingertip, 45–55 minutes. Be sure it cooks to a deep golden brown so it picks up lots of flavour. Let the cake cool in the tin about 10 minutes, then turn it on to a wire rack to cool completely.

Getting Ahead: The longer you keep this cake – up until a week or so – the more moist it will be.

On the Side: Serve in summer with berries, or in winter with *Tropical Fruit Salad in Sweet Wine* (page 155).

In the Glass: Perhaps just coffee will do, but a glass of Italian Vin Santo would also suit the crunchy almonds in this cake.

Serves 6–8

185 g/6½ oz unbleached plain white flour, more for the tin
4 teaspoons baking powder
½ teaspoon salt
125 g/4½ oz coarse yellow cornmeal or polenta
60g/2 oz flaked, blanched almonds
110 g/4 oz butter, diced, more for the tin
200 g/7 oz sugar
2 eggs, lightly beaten
250 ml/8 fl oz Chardonnay white wine

20 cm/8 in springform tin
food processor

BANANA ICE CREAM
(Makes 1 litre/1¾ pints)
Roasting bananas in their skins intensifies the flavour of the fruit.

Heat the oven to 180°C/350°F/Gas Mark 4. Rub the skins of 4 ripe bananas with oil to keep them moist and roast them in a baking dish until dark and soft, 12–15 minutes. Let them cool, then scoop the pulp into a processor and purée it. Beat 4 egg yolks with 200 g/ 7 oz sugar until well mixed, about 1 minute. Next scald 250 ml/8 fl oz double cream with 250 ml/8 fl oz milk and stir it into the egg-yolk mixture. Return this custard to the pan and heat gently, stirring constantly with a wooden spoon, until the custard just coats the back of the spoon (do not let it boil or it will curdle). Take from the heat at once and stir it into the banana purée. Let it cool, then chill it and freeze in an ice-cream churn.

Mocha Chocolate Mousse

It was a wise old chef who taught me this recipe, which gives maximum results for minimum effort. You can vary the coffee flavour here by substituting a different alcohol, such as rum or cognac.

Serves 4

250 g/9 oz dark chocolate
4 egg whites
pinch of salt
2 tablespoons sugar
3 tablespoons double cream
3 tablespoons espresso coffee
3 tablespoons coffee liqueur
cocoa powder, for decoration

4 mousse pots or ramekins
  (175 ml/6 fl oz each)
electric mixer

1 Fill a small saucepan with a 2.5 cm/1 in depth of water and bring to the boil. Chop the chocolate and leave it to melt in a heatproof bowl over the boiling water.

2 Whisk the egg whites with the salt in the mixer until they hold a stiff peak. Add the sugar to make a light meringue, beating until the whites are glossy and hold a long peak, 1–2 minutes. Don't let the meringue wait for more than 5 minutes as it will start to deflate.

3 To make the mocha mixture: bring the cream and coffee to the boil in a small pan and pour it over the chocolate. Let the mixture stand for 15 seconds, then stir until smooth. Take the bowl off the pan of hot water and stir in the coffee liqueur. Add about a quarter of the meringue and stir it until mixed – the heat of the chocolate will lightly cook the meringue. Add to the remaining whites and fold them together as lightly as possible. Spoon the mousse into the mousse pots or ramekins, cover and chill for at least 2 hours until set.

4 Just before serving, top the mousse with a dusting of cocoa.

Getting Ahead: *Mocha Chocolate Mousse* keeps well for up to two days in the refrigerator.

On the Side: A crisp cookie, preferably a home-made 'Small Diversion' (page 164).

In the Glass: Chocolate mousse overwhelms almost everything except a fortified sweet wine such as port or a dark sherry.

Cottage Pudding

Come what may, we always had pudding when I was a child, something sweet and delectable every day. Cottage pudding was one of my favourites, with a hidden surprise of jam, lemon curd or apple sauce in the bottom. It was always baked in the classic English oval pie dish.

1 Heat the oven to 180°C/350°F/Gas Mark 4. Butter the baking dish and spread the jam or lemon curd in the bottom. Sift the flour with the baking powder and salt.
2 Cream the butter in the electric mixer, add the sugar and beat until soft and light, 2–3 minutes. Gradually beat in the eggs, beating well between each addition. Using a rubber spatula, stir in about a third of the flour, followed by half the milk. Add the remaining flour and milk in batches.
3 Spoon the batter into the baking dish and bake in the oven until the pudding is firm in the centre and browned, 50–60 minutes.

Shortcut: Bake the pudding in individual ramekins; it will take only 25–30 minutes.

On the Side: Serve the pudding hot from the oven, with a luxurious touch of *Chateaux* (page 132) as sauce, or an everyday scoop of ice cream.

In the Glass: As a child I must have drunk milk with cottage pudding; now it would be a glass of any simple sweet wine.

Serves 6

225 g/8 oz jam or lemon curd
250 g/9 oz unbleached plain white flour
1¹/₂ teaspoons baking powder
¹/₂ teaspoon salt
110 g/4 oz butter, more for the baking dish
100 g/3¹/₂ oz sugar
2 eggs, whisked to mix
250 ml/8 fl oz milk

medium oval pie dish or 20 cm/8 in round dish, at least 5 cm/2 in deep
electric mixer

Hot or cold, spiced or left plain as you prefer, sautéed cherries must be one of the quickest recipes on record (assuming that you don't remove the stones). When they are served warm over vanilla ice cream, they become Cherries Jubilee, *now an American classic but originally from French cuisine as* cerises jubile. *Figs are equally quick to sauté as a side dish for duck, game birds and foie gras, and they go well with pistachio or coffee ice cream. And in winter, rhubarb comes into play, either with meats such as duck and pork, or as a brisk dessert partner for strawberry or vanilla ice cream.*

Red-wine Cherry Compote (Serves 4)

This compote makes a nice accompaniment to cakes, such as *California Cornmeal Cake* (page 141). Add a teaspoon of ground cinnamon or a tablespoon of grated fresh ginger and you'll have a spiced compote.

675 g/1½ lb cherries
2 tablespoons redcurrant jelly
90 g/3 oz sugar
125 ml/4 fl oz fruity red wine

Stone the cherries, or leave whole, as you prefer. Put the jelly in a large frying pan, add the sugar and heat gently, stirring, until the jelly melts. Add the cherries and cook gently, stirring often, until the juices run – this will take 1–3 minutes, depending on their ripeness. Don't let the cherries boil or they will lose their shape. Pour in the wine, bring just to the boil and then lower the heat and simmer until the cherries are tender, another 1–2 minutes. Check for sweetness and serve hot or cold.

Roast Rhubarb with Port (Serves 4–6)

Cut 675 g/1½ lb rhubarb in 5 cm/2 in sticks and spread them in a baking dish so they all touch the bottom. Sprinkle them with 150 g/5½ oz sugar, or more if you like your rhubarb sweet. Mix 175 ml/6 fl oz ruby port with the grated zest of 1 orange and pour it over the rhubarb. Roast it uncovered in a 180°C/350°F/Gas Mark 4 oven until just tender when pierced with a knife, 20–30 minutes. (With careful cooking, it is possible to keep rhubarb pieces whole but they will dissolve to purée if overdone.) Serve the rhubarb warm or chilled over ice cream.

Sautéed Caramelized Figs (Serves 4–6)

Halve 450 g/1 lb figs and dip the cut sides in about 75 g/2½ oz sugar. Sauté them, cut sides down, in 45–60 g/1½–2 oz hot butter until the sugar caramelizes, 4–6 minutes. Take them out, deglaze the pan juices with 175 ml/4 fl oz Marsala or port and pour the juices over the figs.

Red-wine Cherry Compote

Do you know anyone who does not have a stash of bought ice creams hidden away in their freezer? I don't. Fine for a mid-afternoon snack, but can I suggest you might add something more personal at table? How about a hot honey chocolate sauce for vanilla ice cream, or a refreshing burst of orange and lemon with strawberry? My own particular favourite is a fresh mango sauce for sorbets.

Ready-made ice cream can be a useful basis for your own flavourings. Simply allow the ice cream to soften so it can be stirred, add toasted nuts, candied fruits, melted chocolate, alcohol such as rum, whatever strikes your fancy or your cupboard can supply, and refreeze the mixture. You'll find a couple of ideas here as just a start and a frivolous topping – candied rose petals.

Orange Lemon Sauce

(Makes 250 ml/8 fl oz, serves 4)

A warm sauce, perfect for fruit ice creams, particularly strawberry. Delicious with cakes too.

Grate the zest from 1 orange and 1 lemon, and then squeeze the juice. Mix 1 tablespoon cornflour into 100 g/3½ oz sugar in a saucepan and stir in 125 ml/4 fl oz water and the orange and lemon juices. Bring to the boil, stirring constantly until the sauce thickens. Take from the heat and stir in the grated citrus zest and 2 tablespoons butter, cut in pieces. Serve as soon as possible to retain the citrus freshness.

Mango Sauce

(Makes 375 ml/12 fl oz, serves 4)

A refreshing cold sauce to serve with fruit sorbet.

Peel 2 ripe mangoes (about 750 g/1¾ lb) and cut the flesh from the stones. Purée the flesh in a processor or blender and work in the juice of 1 lemon or lime and 2–3 tablespoons icing sugar. Taste, add 1–2 tablespoons rum if you like, and adjust the amount of sugar.

Ginger Cookie Ice Cream

(Serves 4)

As I love ginger cookies, here's my sneaky treat.

Make or buy 1 litre/1¾ pints vanilla ice cream and leave it to soften so it can be stirred. Put 60 g/2 oz ginger cookies in a plastic bag and pound with a rolling pin until they are coarsely crushed. Stir the crumbs into the ice cream and freeze until firm.

Chocolate Honey Sauce

(Makes 250 ml/8 fl oz, serves 4)

Memorable with a spiced ice cream such as cinnamon or ginger, or just plain vanilla.

In a saucepan, mix 30 g/1 oz chopped unsweetened chocolate, 30 g/1 oz chopped dark chocolate, 3 heaped tablespoons honey, 125 ml/4 fl oz double cream and the grated zest of 1 orange. Stir over low heat until the chocolate has melted, then bring the sauce to the boil and simmer until it thickens enough to coat the back of a spoon, 2–3 minutes. Take from the heat and, if you like, stir in a tablespoon of rum.

Eskimo Ice Cream

(Serves 6)

When our children were small, we lived in France and their favourite treat was an 'Eskimo', ice cream coated with chocolate on a stick. This is a grown-up version.

Make or buy 1 litre/1¾ pints vanilla ice cream and let it soften so it can be stirred. Stir in 75 g/2½ oz dried raisins, 110 g/4 oz chopped dried apricots, and 200 g/7 oz coarsely chopped nuts such as walnuts. If you use hazelnuts, almonds or pine nuts, they should be toasted for the best flavour (page 166). Pack the mixture into six individual ramekins, smoothing the top. Freeze it until firm. Melt 110 g/4 oz dark chocolate, allowing about a tablespoon per person, trail it in a lattice over the ice cream and freeze again. Serve directly in the moulds from the freezer. Perfect on a hot day.

Candied mint leaves or rose petals

These add just the right wisp of colour to a pale ice cream or delicate mousse.

Lightly whisk an egg white in a small bowl just until broken up. Brush both sides of the mint leaves, or the upper side of a pink rose petal, lightly with egg white. Dip mint sprigs in sugar, or lightly sprinkle rose petals. Coarse sugar, if you have it, will be prettiest. Place well apart on a sheet of non-stick baking paper and leave to crispen in a dry place, 1–2 hours. Candied like this, they keep for 4–6 hours, or dry for several hours in a very low oven with the door open, they will be dry enough to store in an airtight container for at least a month.

TIPS FOR CHOCOLATE SAUCE

A shot of alcohol improves ready-made chocolate sauce like nothing else: whisk in 1–2 tablespoons rum, whisky or brandy, adding it just before serving so the alcohol has no time to evaporate.

For a fluffy chocolate sauce, heat the sauce and stir in some marshmallows, snipping them in four with scissors and allowing one marshmallow per person. Warm the sauce, stirring until the marshmallows are melted.

For crisp texture, stir an equal volume of rice cereal into your favourite hot chocolate sauce and serve at once.

Mars bars make a killer sauce for ice cream. Cut the bars in cubes, allowing a regular bar per person, and add 3–4 tablespoons milk per bar. Heat the bars in a bowl in a bath of hot water, stirring until melted.

Flambéed fruits are culinary theatre, to be presented live at the last minute, preferably in front of guests in the kitchen or at table over a portable burner. As well as providing a thrill, flambéed fruit tastes delicious; it can be served alone with sponge fingers or petits fours, but is best of all spooned on top of crêpes or ice cream.

Roast Brandied Plums with Ginger

(Serves 6)

Plums are an underrated fruit, I think. The purple *quetsches* from the crabbed old tree in our garden are hearteningly juicy and full flavoured, especially roasted in Burgundian fashion in blackcurrant syrup, then flamed with brandy. Any kind of plum can be roasted in this way, and apricots and peaches are equally delicious. Either non-alcoholic blackcurrant cordial, or Cassis blackcurrant liqueur are good for the syrup.

675 g/1½ lb plums
125 ml/4 fl oz blackcurrant cordial or cassis
60 ml/2 fl oz brandy

For the stuffing

60 g/2 oz dry biscuits, such as Rich Tea
60 g/2 oz butter, at room temperature
60 g/2 oz dark brown sugar
60 g/2 oz candied or crystallized ginger, chopped

Heat the oven to 200°C/400°F/Gas Mark 6. Rinse and dry the plums. Next, run a knife halfway along their indentation, then scoop out and discard the stones, leaving a pocket in the fruit.

Make the stuffing: crumble the biscuits with your fingers, or crush them in a bowl with the end of a rolling pin. Using an electric mixer, cream the butter with the sugar, then stir in the biscuit crumbs and the ginger.

Push small mounds of the stuffing into the plums. Set them in a baking dish and spoon over the blackcurrant cordial or cassis. Roast the plums in the oven, basting them regularly, until they are tender and one or two skins have split; 10–15 minutes depending on their size and ripeness. (Large or underripe plums can take twice as long.)

Remove the plums from the oven. Heat the brandy in a small pan until it just starts to bubble. Set it alight and stand back from the flames. Pour the flaming brandy over the plums and baste them until the flames die. Serve them hot or at room temperature.

Apples Flambéed with Calvados

(Serves 4)

Serve these apples as dessert or as an accompaniment to roast duck or pork.

Peel, core and slice 4 tart apples into crescents. Next melt 60 g/2 oz butter in a frying pan over medium–high heat, add the apples and sprinkle with 2 tablespoons sugar. Turn them, sprinkle with 1–2 tablespoons more sugar, and fry them briskly until caramelized and tender, turning so that they brown evenly and thoroughly, 8–12 minutes. Add 60 ml/2 fl oz Calvados and flambé it. Baste until the flames die, and serve at once.

Bananas Flambéed with Rum

(Serves 4)

Served over vanilla ice cream, these flamed bananas become *Bananas Foster*, the New Orleans speciality.

Peel and slice 4 bananas lengthwise. Melt 60 g/2 oz butter in a frying pan. Add 60 g/2 oz brown sugar and heat gently, stirring until the sugar has melted, about 2 minutes. Add the bananas and cook until caramelized, 3–5 minutes, turning once. Sprinkle with cinnamon. Pour 75 ml/2½ fl oz rum over the bananas and flambé them, basting the fruit with the sauce until the flames subside. Serve immediately.

Flambéed Peaches with Kirsch

(Serves 4)

Serve the peaches alone, sprinkled with chopped pecans, or make peach shortcakes. Spoon the hot peaches over split shortcakes, top with whipped cream and serve at once.

Peel 4 freestone peaches: pour boiling water over the peaches in a bowl, leave 10 seconds and drain them. Run a knife around the indentation and twist peaches in half, discarding the stone. Strip off the skin. Leave peaches as halves, or cut in crescents, as you prefer. Sauté in butter and brown sugar as for bananas. Flambé with 75 ml/2½ fl oz kirsch.

TIPS FOR FLAMBÉED FRUIT

First sauté the fruit in butter and sugar until the fruit is tender and caramelized. (A tablespoon of butter and sugar per serving of fruit is a good benchmark.) Baste the fruit with the syrup produced by the fruit juices.

Pour in the alcohol, allowing 1–2 tablespoons per serving – not too much as the flames can be fierce. Brandy and rum blend with almost any fruit, while kirsch, the cherry-based *eau de vie*, suits stone fruits like plums, peaches and of course cherries themselves.

Hold a lit match to the side of the pan, or carefully tilt the edge of the pan over a gas flame so that the flame just catches the alcohol. It is important to set it alight just as it comes to boiling point. If the alcohol doesn't flame it may not have been hot enough, or it may have overheated so the alcohol has already evaporated. Baste the fruit with the juices until the flames die, then serve at once.

The very best desserts, whether towering hot soufflés, moulded jellies or a golden caramelized fruit tart, will always catch the eye of your guests. The drama continues as the spoon slides into the soufflé, or the knife dissects the crispy pastry. At last comes the high note of the first, luscious spoonful. I love my desserts to be a grand finale, and here you'll find some prime performers.

Dessert must not fade into insignificance after the impact of previous courses. Its taste and texture must be distinctive. First I look for bold flavours – the tang of citrus, the intensity of chocolate. I've noticed that a shot of wine or spirits rarely comes amiss. Mixtures such as zabaglione must be feather-light and creams must be satin-smooth; the crunch of pastry such as filo is much appreciated.

One important attribute of a good dessert is distinctive presentation. The brilliant colour of red berries and the golden and green hues of tropical fruits give you a head start. Then comes careful treatment of the ingredients – the neat slices of pear in a tart, with the halves lined up to resemble a flower, or the amusement of chocolate 'salami' arranged on a stark white plate. The choice of serving dish, whether stemmed glass for an ice cream or mousse, or giant flat platter to frame a tart, all adds to the sense of occasion.

All of these desserts are designed for special occasions, for a dinner party or perhaps an anniversary. You'll see that with the single exception of *Hot Strawberry Soufflés*, they can be made ahead. One or two may need a bit of last-minute assembly with whipped cream, but the array of fruit tarts, *Red-wine Tart*, *Peppered Pears in Red Wine* and my special chilled version of zabaglione can all be finished hours in advance, ready to go. That's my idea of a happy ending for myself as cook, as well as my guests!

Happy Endings

Hot Strawberry Soufflés

I love to experiment with soufflés, balancing just the right amount of fluffy egg white with an intensely flavoured base, firm enough to support the whites without being heavy. Here strawberries are simply puréed with sugar, then folded with meringue – a startlingly simple mixture that dates back over two centuries to Chef Antonin Carême, who cooked for the Russian Tsar Alexander I, the British Prince Regent and the Prince de Talleyrand, who masterminded the Congress of Vienna. Star chefs are nothing new!

1 Heat the oven to 200°C/400°F/Gas Mark 6. Hull the strawberries and purée them in a blender or food processor. Stir in half of the sugar, adding more to taste depending on their sweetness. Brush the ramekins generously with melted butter.

2 Stiffly whisk the egg whites, stir in the remaining sugar and continue whisking until the whites are glossy and hold a long peak, about a minute. Stir about a quarter of this meringue into the strawberry mixture to lighten it. Add this to the remaining egg whites and fold them together as lightly as possible.

3 Spoon the soufflé mixture into the prepared ramekins and smooth the top. Run your thumb around the edge of the soufflés so they rise in a hat shape. Set them on a baking sheet and bake in the oven until puffed and brown, 10–12 minutes. When gently shaken they should wobble slightly but not much.

4 Sprinkle the soufflés with icing sugar and set them on napkins or paper doilies on individual plates so they do not slip. Rush them to the table.

Serves 6

225 g/8 oz strawberries
100 g/3^{1}/2 oz sugar, more if needed
melted butter for the ramekins
5 egg whites
icing sugar, for sprinkling

6 ramekins (250 ml/8 fl oz capacity each)

Getting Ahead: *Strawberry Soufflés* could hardly be quicker to make, but they have one disadvantage – they cannot be prepared ahead.

On the Side: More strawberries – I'd recommend slicing them, then stirring in 1–2 tablespoons of sugar and a tablespoon of Grand Marnier. Serve a crisp cookie on the side, perhaps chosen from my 'Small Diversions' (page 164).

In the Glass: A well risen soufflé surely deserves a toast in Champagne.

Venetian Chilled Zabaglione with Sparkling White Wine

Traditional zabaglione is flavoured with Marsala, but I prefer this delicate Venetian version made with the pleasantly dry local sparkling white Prosecco. You'll find Prosecco at many good wine stores, or any medium-dry sparkling wine can be substituted.

Serves 6

150 ml/5 fl oz dry sparkling white wine
  such as Prosecco
1 teaspoon powdered gelatine
8 egg yolks
90 g/3 oz sugar
250 ml/8 fl oz double cream
110 g/4 oz bar of dark chocolate
  (for decoration)

6 glasses (250 ml/8 fl oz each)

1 Put about 2 tablespoons of the wine in a very small pan, sprinkle over the gelatine and leave for about 5 minutes until spongy.
2 Put the yolks, sugar and remaining wine in a heatproof bowl and set it over a pan of hot but not boiling water. Whisk vigorously with a balloon whisk or hand-held electric mixer. The zabaglione will froth and lighten in colour, then thicken gradually until it leaves a trail for about 5 seconds when the whisk is lifted. This process should take at least 5 minutes so the mousse thickens to a close, smooth texture; if it starts to thicken too fast, take it from the heat so it cooks more slowly.
3 Take the bowl off the heat. Warm the pan of gelatine over the pan of hot water until the gelatine has melted and then whisk it into the warm mousse. Set the bowl over ice and whisk until cold, 5–7 minutes. Whisk the cream until it holds a soft peak, then fold it into the cold mousse mixture. Pour the zabaglione into the glasses, cover and chill for at least 2 hours until the zabaglione is lightly set.
4 For the decoration, leave the chocolate bar at room temperature for 1 hour. Using a vegetable peeler, shave several curls from the side of the bar. Sprinkle them over the zabaglione just before serving. (You'll find these curls useful for decorating all sorts of desserts.)

Getting Ahead: This holds up happily for 12 hours or more, whereas most zabaglione recipes must be made at the last minute.

On the Side: Fresh fruits are a happy addition to *Venetian Zabaglione*. Drop some fresh strawberries, raspberries or other berries into the glasses before pouring it in.

In the Glass: More of that agreeable Prosecco that slips down so easily.

Raspberry Mint Jellies

This is a colourful, refreshing little dessert for summer, much loved by anyone with childhood memories of Jello. Most berries are good with mint and so can take the place of raspberries; larger ones such as strawberries should be sliced. The dramatic dark colours of the mint and berries are set off by the crystal jelly.

Serves 4

15 g/^{1}/$_2$ oz gelatine
500 ml/16 fl oz water
medium bunch of mint (about 40 g/1^1/$_2$ oz)
170 g/6 oz sugar
2 tablespoons white alcohol (framboise or kirsch)
225 g/8 oz raspberries

4 ramekins or glasses (175 ml/6 fl oz
  capacity each)

1 Sprinkle the gelatine over 3–4 tablespoons of the water in a medium bowl and leave until spongy, at least 5 minutes. Choose four pretty mint leaves and reserve four sprigs for decoration. Put the rest, with the stems, in a saucepan with the sugar and remaining water. Heat until the sugar dissolves, cover and bring the syrup to the boil. Leave it to infuse over low heat for 10–15 minutes. Meanwhile, blanch the four mint leaves to set their colour: bring a small pan of water to the boil, add the mint leaves and bring just back to the boil. Drain and rinse with cold water, draining thoroughly.

2 Strain the syrup and add it to the softened gelatine and stir until melted. Stir in the alcohol.

3 Set the ramekins or glasses in a roasting pan of iced water. Pour 1 tablespoon of mint jelly into each ramekin and leave until just set, 3–5 minutes. Lay a mint leaf on the jelly and cover with two more tablespoons jelly, again leaving just until set, 3–5 minutes more. Top with the raspberries, pressing down slightly. Fill with the remaining jelly, taking care to cover the raspberries completely. Cover and leave in the refrigerator to set, 4–6 hours.

4 To serve: if using ramekins, dip each one for 3–5 seconds in warm water, loosen the jelly from the sides of the mould and turn it on to a chilled plate. Alternatively, serve jelly in the glasses. Decorate with a mint sprig.

Getting Ahead: The jellies keep well in the refrigerator for up to two days. After a few hours the gelatine will stiffen, so if you are preparing ahead, let the jellies soften at room temperature for an hour before serving.

On the Side: On a hot day *Raspberry Mint Jellies* are good plain, or you may like to add a spoonful of clotted cream, whipped cream or crème fraîche.

In the Glass: On a warm evening, here's the place for a sweet sparkling wine such as a Vouvray.

Peppered Pears in Red Wine

Pears and red wine are natural partners. When you immerse pears in a warm infusion of spices and red wine, they start to blush at once, absorbing the colour and heady taste of the wine. Peppered pears have the same tantalizing aroma, the same lingering tingle of taste as mulled wine – perfect on a cold winter day. When chilled, they take on another dimension, a complexity that spells dinner party to me. Firm pears that keep their shape are important for poaching; Anjou, Packham or Conference do well.

Serves 4

1 tablespoon Sichuan peppercorns
1 tablespoon black peppercorns
pared zest of 1 lemon
90 g/3 oz sugar, more if needed
1 bottle (750 ml) red wine
4–6 large pears (about 1 kg/2¼ lb), with stems
4–6 mint sprigs

1 Tie the Sichuan and black peppercorns with the lemon zest in a piece of muslin and put them in a deep medium saucepan with the sugar and wine. Heat gently until the sugar dissolves, then cover, bring to the boil and leave the syrup to infuse over low heat for 10–15 minutes.

2 Peel the pears with a vegetable peeler, leaving the stems, and scoop out the flower indentation with the tip of the peeler. (Leaving the stems on makes them easy to handle using the stem, and more attractive for serving.) With a melon ball cutter or teaspoon, scoop out the core inside the pear, leaving it whole. Cut a thin slice from the base of the pear so it sits upright. At once drop the pear into wine syrup so it is moistened and does not discolour. Repeat with the remaining pears. Add enough water to cover them and set a heatproof plate on top so they remain immersed and don't form a 'tideline'.

3 Bring the pears slowly to the boil and poach them until translucent and tender when pierced with the point of a knife, 10–25 minutes. Timing varies very much with ripeness. Let the pears cool to tepid, then transfer them to a bowl with a draining spoon.

4 Boil the wine syrup until concentrated and slightly thickened, 15–25 minutes, depending on how much water was added. About 300 ml/10 fl oz of syrup should be left. Strain the syrup over the pears, discarding the bag of spices. The pears can be served hot, at room temperature or chilled, and at each stage their flavour will differ.

5 To serve hot: warm the pears in a covered pan on top of the stove. Set a scoop of ice cream in each bowl, flatten it and set a pear upright on top. Spoon over the hot syrup, add a mint sprig and serve at once.

6 To serve cold: set the chilled pears upright in shallow individual bowls with the syrup spooned on top. Decorate the bowl with mint sprigs.

Shortcut: Instead of leaving the pears whole after peeling, quarter them and scoop out the cores and central stem. Poach the quarters in the syrup without added water – they will take only 8–12 minutes and the wine syrup will reduce much more quickly.

Getting Ahead: If you can, store the peppered pears overnight, or up to two days, in the refrigerator – they will colour even more and their flavour will intensify.

On the Side: *Peppered Pears* can be set on a circle of sponge cake to absorb the wine syrup, or flanked by your favourite shortbread or biscotti.

In the Glass: *Peppered Pears* are a compelling invitation to a glass of port or one of those dense, languorous Muscats from southern France, California or Australia.

Tropical Fruit Salad in Sweet Wine

When I was 16, I made a fruit salad very like this one for my parents. They gave it the royal treatment – cut-glass bowl, silver spoon and a bottle of sweet, late-picked wine. Ever since it's been a speciality of mine and I ring the changes of fruit and wine according to the season. The main aim is to unite fruits of contrasting colours and textures so their flavours blend. For a non-alcoholic fruit salad, you could substitute pineapple or apple juice for the wine.

1 Heat the sugar with the water over low heat until the sugar dissolves. Bring the syrup to the boil and simmer for 2 minutes. Pour the syrup into a large bowl and leave it to cool.
2 Peel the papayas, cut them in half and scoop out the seeds. Cut each half crosswise into slices and immerse them in the sugar syrup – this stops them from discolouring.
3 For the mangoes, use a sharp knife to cut off the flesh on either side of the stone. Then slash the flesh into large chunks, cutting to the peel, but not through it. Push the centre of the peel with your thumbs to turn it inside out so the cubes stick up from the peel. Cut them from the peel and add to the syrup.
4 Peel the tangerines and pull them in half. Cut the tangerine halves crosswise, then pull the segments apart and add them, with the grapes, to the other fruits in the syrup.
5 Pour in the wine and stir gently to mix the fruit. Taste the salad and if needed, add lime or lemon juice. Cover the bowl with clingfilm and leave in the refrigerator for at least 3 hours so the flavours develop.
6 Just before serving, cut off the tops of the passion fruit, scoop out the seeds and stir them into the salad.

Shortcut: Use only two or three fruits instead of five.

Getting Ahead: A 12- or even 24-hour rest in the refrigerator will do fruit salad no harm.

On the Side: With fresh fruit salad, it's hard to beat double cream, plus a piece of shortbread.

In the Glass: One of the many late-picked sweet Rieslings that are being made in California, New York and Australia as well as Alsace would be ideal.

Serves 6

90 g/3 oz sugar

125 ml/4 fl oz water

2 small papayas

2 medium mangoes

4 seedless tangerines or other loose-skinned oranges

140 g/5 oz green grapes, seedless if possible

140 g/5 oz red grapes, seedless if possible

300 ml/10 fl oz sweet white wine

squeeze of lime or lemon juice

2 passion fruit

Cherry Almond Tart

You will find many of the ingredients for this tart in your cupboard. An electric mixer or processor makes this an easy recipe to prepare.

1 Make the pastry, wrap and chill it (page 165). Roll out the dough, line the tart tin and chill for 15 minutes. Heat the oven to 190°C/375°F/Gas Mark 5 and set a baking sheet low down in the oven to heat so the base of the tart cooks thoroughly.

2 For the almond filling: cream the butter in an electric mixer or processor, add the sugar and salt and beat vigorously until the mixture is light and soft. Gradually beat in the egg and egg yolk. Lastly, stir in the ground almonds and stir by hand or use the processor pulse button, taking care not to over-mix or the oil will be drawn out of the almonds, making the filling heavy. Spread the almond filling in the pastry case. Stone the cherries using a cherry stoner or the tip of a vegetable peeler. Arrange the cherries, stem-end down, in concentric circles on the filling. (If you start at the edge of the tart, it's easier to get concentric circles.) Chill the tart for 10–15 minutes.

3 Set the tart in the oven on the heated baking sheet and bake until the pastry is brown and starts to pull from the sides of the pan, 35–45 minutes. The filling will puff around the cherries and brown too. Let the tart cool on a wire rack.

4 To unmould the tart, set it on an upturned bowl so that the tin rim slips down over the bowl. Using a metal spatula, slide the tart from the base on to a flat serving plate – be sure the serving plate is flat so the tart does not crack. Just before serving, lightly sprinkle the tart with icing sugar and serve it warm or at room temperature.

Getting Ahead: Try this tart the next day, when it will be moister and richer.

On the Side: A scoop of vanilla ice cream or single cream is always welcome, though by no means necessary.

In the Glass: A cherry almond tart invites a glass of sweet Muscat such as a Beaumes-de-Venise.

Serves 8

450 g/1 lb cherries
icing sugar, for sprinkling

For the sweet shortcrust pastry

90 g/3 oz sugar
3 egg yolks
1 teaspoon vanilla extract
90 g/3 oz butter, softened
185 g/6$^{1}/_{2}$ oz unbleached plain white flour
$^{1}/_{2}$ teaspoon salt

For the almond filling

110 g/4 oz butter, softened
100 g/3$^{1}/_{2}$ oz sugar
pinch of salt
1 egg and 1 egg yolk, beaten to mix
110 g/4 oz ground almonds
icing sugar, to decorate

22 cm/9 in tart tin with removable base

Red-wine Tart

I came across this unusual red-wine tart in an old Burgundian cookbook. It causes amusement at table as the filling looks like chocolate, so the first burst of wine, backed by cinnamon, comes as a shock. Red-wine Tart is clearly designed to use a light, fruity red wine (if Pinot Noir is beyond your budget, a Beaujolais or Gamay does fine) and calls for just five ingredients in the filling. My kind of recipe!

Serves 4–6

2 eggs

90 g/3 oz sugar

2 teaspoons cornflour

2 teaspoons ground cinnamon

250 ml/8 fl oz fruity red wine

icing sugar, for dusting

175 ml/6 fl oz double cream, lightly
   whipped, to decorate

For the sweet shortcrust pastry

90 g/3 oz sugar

3 egg yolks

1 teaspoon vanilla extract

90 g/3 oz butter, softened

185 g/6^{1}/$_2$ oz unbleached plain white
   flour

^{1}/$_2$ teaspoon salt

22 cm/9 in tart tin with removable base

1 Make the sweet shortcrust pastry (page 165) and chill for 15 minutes. Roll out the dough, line the tart tin and chill the pastry case for at least 15 minutes until firm. Heat the oven to 190°C/375°F/Gas Mark 5.

2 Heat a baking sheet low down in the oven. Line the pastry case with foil, fill with dry beans or rice, and bake it blind (page 166). Turn the oven down to 180°C/350°F/Gas Mark 4.

3 Whisk the eggs with the sugar, cornflour and cinnamon until just mixed (don't let a froth form as this will spoil the smooth surface of the tart). Stir in the wine. Pour the filling into the pastry shell and bake until set, 20–25 minutes. Cool the tart in the tin for 5 minutes, then set it on an upturned bowl, let the rim fall off and leave the tart, on the base, on a rack to cool completely.

4 Shortly before serving, sprinkle the tart with icing sugar and slide it from the base on to a flat platter. Serve a spoonful of cream with each piece of tart.

Getting Ahead: *Red-wine Tart* can be baked and kept for 6–8 hours before serving. Keep it covered at room temperature and add the icing sugar and cream just before serving.

On the Side: Possibly some more whipped cream.

In the Glass: A rich sweet wine such as a ruby port or dark oloroso sherry.

Saffron Apple Tart

Just a pinch of saffron perfumes this whole tart and, when you see the glowing golden colour, you'll appreciate why saffron is the world's most valuable spice, ounce for ounce more costly than gold.

1 Roll out the dough, line the tart tin and chill for 15–30 minutes (page 166). Heat the oven to 190°C/375°F/Gas Mark 5 and put a baking sheet low down to heat.
2 For the filling: heat the milk with the honey to boiling, stirring until the honey is melted. Remove from the heat, sprinkle over the saffron and leave it to soak for at least 15 minutes.
3 Spread the raisins in the pastry case. Peel, quarter, and core the apples, then cut the quarters in crescents – the thinner they are, the prettier the tart will be. Arrange the slices overlapping in concentric circles. Whisk the eggs until mixed and stir in the cooled milk mixture. Pour it over the apples.
4 Set the tart in the oven on the heated baking sheet and bake until the filling is set and lightly browned, 35–45 minutes. The apples should be tender and the pastry should shrink slightly from the sides of the pan. Cool the tart in the tin for 5 minutes, then set it on an upturned bowl so that the tin rim slips down over the bowl. Using a metal spatula, slide the tart from the base on to a flat serving plate.

Shortcut: Instead of bothering to arrange the apples in circles, halve and core them, then dice them including the peel and spread them on the raisins in the shell. Add the filling and bake as described.

Getting Ahead: This is a tart that keeps well, so you can bake it early in the day for the evening.

On the Side: Serve the tart warm, with ice cream or crème fraîche.

In the Glass: White wine with some body and sweetness, a Sémillon or Gewürztraminer, would be my choice.

Serves 6–8

175 ml/6 fl oz milk
2 heaped tablespoons honey
large pinch of saffron strands
110 g/4 oz raisins
3 Granny Smith apples (about 450 g/1 lb)
3 eggs
450 g/1 lb bought puff pastry dough

22 cm/9 in tart tin with removable base

Apple and Cream Cheese Strudel

I've long ago given up making strudel dough, now that sheets of frozen filo are readily available in the supermarket. Filo provides all of the crispness of strudel with none of the hard work of rolling and stretching the dough to paper thinness. For a crowd, make two or three rolls of strudel, doubling or tripling the filling and using more of the many sheets of pastry that come in a package.

Serves 4–6

3 tart apples (about 450 g/1 lb)

90 g/3 oz butter, melted

60 g/2 oz brown sugar

grated zest of 1 lemon

1 teaspoon ground cinnamon (optional)

225 g/8 oz Philadelphia cream cheese

1 egg

1–2 tablespoons cream

5 sheets filo pastry (about 90 g/3 oz)

60 g/2 oz walnut pieces

icing sugar, for sprinkling

1 Heat the oven to 190°C/375°F/Gas Mark 5. Peel, core and thinly slice the apples. Butter a baking sheet. Mix the sugar, lemon zest and cinnamon if using, in a small bowl and divide the mixture in half. Beat one half into the cream cheese, then beat in the egg. If the cheese mixture is too stiff to spread, beat in some cream.

2 Lay a dry tea towel on the work surface, short-side nearest to you. Unwrap the filo pastry and lay a sheet on the towel, short-side nearest to you (filo pastry dries quickly in the open air, so keep the remaining sheets covered with a slightly dampened cloth while you are working). Brush the sheet with melted butter, lay another sheet on top and brush this also with butter. Spread the cream cheese mixture as evenly as possible on the dough. Brush two more sheets of dough with butter and lay them over the cheese. Sprinkle them with the remaining sugar mixture and scatter with the sliced apples. Add a last layer of buttered filo and sprinkle it with the walnuts. (Leftover filo can be tightly wrapped and frozen to use another time.)

3 Fold the corners of dough nearest to you inwards about 2.5 cm/1 in. Pull upwards on the edge of the towel nearest to you so the pastry rolls into quite a tight cylinder. Transfer the roll to the buttered baking sheet, seam-side down. Brush the roll with butter. Bake the strudel in the oven until crisp and brown and a skewer inserted in the centre is hot to the touch when withdrawn, 20–25 minutes.

4 Serve the strudel hot or at room temperature. Just before serving, sprinkle it generously with icing sugar and cut it in four diagonal slices with a serrated knife (the trimmings are the cook's perks!).

Getting Ahead: The strudel can be prepared and refrigerated up to 6 hours before you bake it. It is best still warm from the oven, but you can also cook it up to 8 hours ahead and then warm it just before serving.

On the Side: A bowl of whipped Chantilly cream flavoured with cognac or vanilla and a tablespoon of sugar.

In the Cup: Your favourite coffee.

Macadamia Nut Cake with Dark Chocolate

One of my Australian students, Jenny Richardson, owns a macadamia farm and here's her surprising recipe for macadamia nut cake, laced with dark chocolate. The batter rises like a sponge cake even though it has very little flour. If your macadamias are salted (most of them are), rinse them with cold water, drain thoroughly and dry them in a 120°C/250°F/Gas Mark 1/2 oven for 5 minutes. The nuts have an oil content of over 70%, most of it unsaturated, so the cake is wonderfully rich. Don't be tempted to buy macadamias in their shells – they are almost impossible to crack without a machine!

1 Heat the oven to 160°C/325°F/Gas Mark 3. Set aside 2 tablespoons of the chocolate for topping. In a processor, grind half of the nuts with 3 tablespoons of the sugar and stir the mixture into the remaining chocolate. Grind the remaining nuts with 3 tablespoons more sugar and add to the chocolate mixture. (Grinding the nuts in small quantities with sugar helps prevent the oil from separating and making the cake heavy.) Sift the flour and baking powder and add to the chocolate mixture. Butter the cake tin, line the base with non-stick baking paper and butter the paper. Sprinkle the pan with a bit more flour, discarding the excess.

2 In the mixer, beat the egg yolks with 3–4 tablespoons of the remaining sugar until the mixture is thick and holds a ribbon trail, about 3 minutes. Then in a separate bowl, whisk the egg whites until stiff, add the remaining sugar and continue whisking until glossy, about 1 minute. Fold about a third of the macadamia mixture into the egg-yolk mixture. Add about a third of the egg whites and fold together also. Continue folding in macadamias and egg whites in two more batches.

3 Spoon the batter into the cake tin, smooth the top and tap the tin on the counter to burst any air bubbles. Bake the cake in the oven until a skewer inserted in the centre comes out clean, 45–50 minutes. Let the cake cool slightly, then remove the tin sides and slide off the base; peel off the paper. Sprinkle the warm top of the cake with reserved chocolate so it melts and forms an attractive speckled top. Leave it to cool and set.

Getting Ahead: This cake is money in the bank. It keeps well in an airtight container for at least a week, perfect for cutting a quick slice from time to time, and the flavour continues to mellow.

On the Side: On the top you might want to add some plump strawberries, half dipped in melted chocolate so they stick to the cake.

In the Glass: Let's stay in Australia with one of their famous 'stickies', white wines of honeyed intensity. Or if you prefer less sugar, I'd go for a powerful Australian red Shiraz.

Makes a 23 cm/9 in cake, to serve 6–8

75 g/2¹/₂ oz dark chocolate, finely chopped
330 g/12 oz unsalted macadamia nuts
150 g/5¹/₂ oz sugar
30 g/1 oz unbleached plain white flour, more
  for dusting the tin
¹/₂ teaspoon baking powder
butter for the tin
5 eggs, separated

23 cm/9 in springform tin
electric mixer

Chocolate Salami

Dark chocolate and hazelnuts are the basis of this recipe, a natural pair known in Italian by the single name gianduia. *I came across this 'salami' – or* Budino Gianduia *– in a rural trattoria when the owner cut a few slices from a roll resembling the familiar sausage and urged us to try it with our apéritifs. Chocolate salami can be dressed up for a dinner party, or down to slice as a quick treat for children. Dry biscuits, on the lines of Rich Tea, are needed to make the salami, and it keeps for weeks. If you have a triangular bar cookie mould (575-ml/1-pint capacity), a triangular 'salami' makes an unusual and visually striking presentation.*

Serves 6

40 g/1¹/₂ oz hazelnuts
60 g/2 oz dry biscuits
1 egg
1 egg yolk
100 g/3¹/₂ oz sugar
75 g/2¹/₂ oz butter
75 g/2¹/₂ oz dark chocolate, chopped

For decoration

250 ml/8 fl oz double cream, stiffly whipped
225 g/8 oz berries, e.g. strawberries or
  raspberries, prepared

electric mixer
triangular bar cookie mould (575-ml/1-pint
  capacity), optional

1 Toast and peel the hazelnuts (page 166). Place in a plastic bag and pound with a heavy pan or rolling pin to crush them. Break the biscuits, put in a plastic bag and crush. If using a mould, line it with non-stick baking paper.
2 Beat the egg, egg yolk and sugar in an electric mixer until light and thick, about 5 minutes. Meanwhile melt the butter and chocolate in a medium bowl over a water bath, stirring occasionally until the mixture is smooth. Stir in the egg-yolk mixture and cook in the water bath, stirring constantly, until hot to the touch, 4–5 minutes; the mixture will thicken slightly. Take it from the heat and stir in the hazelnuts and biscuits.
3 Let it cool until firm enough to shape, then turn on to a sheet of non-stick baking paper and shape to a 5-cm/2-in cylinder. Wrap tightly and chill. If using a biscuit mould, transfer to the lined mould, pressing it in to exclude air bubbles. Cover and leave at room temperature until set, ¹/₂–1 hour.
4 To finish: if chilling the salami for more than 2 hours, let it return to room temperature before slicing. With a thin, sharp knife cut it into 18 triangles or rounds. Arrange three slices on individual plates, with some cream and berries.

Shortcut: Substitute blanched almonds for the hazelnuts and you'll be saved the bother of peeling the nuts.

Getting Ahead: *Chocolate Salami* can be stored in the refrigerator for two weeks, or frozen for three months. Let it come to room temperature before slicing it.

On the Side: I have two favourite arrangements for *Chocolate Salami* on the plate. One is a wigwam of three triangles propped on a large rosette of whipped cream and garnished with berries. The other is a Christmas tree shaped with three overlapping triangles and a sliver of salami as stem. Raspberries decorate the 'branches', with a silver ball at the top of the tree. Other decorations can include your choice of whole strawberries, orange segments, candied orange peel, Cape gooseberries, chocolate coins, chocolate truffles or Baci candies.

In the Glass: Look for one of those typical Italian apéritifs – Campari, Cynar or vermouth – to accompany a slice or two of *Chocolate Salami*. For a more serious serving as dessert, a sweet wine such as Vin Santo would be perfect.

French Walnut Galette

Here's another outlet for ready-made filo pastry, a delicious flaky galette flavoured with walnuts, apples and Armagnac. It comes from Gascony in western France, where it is known as Feuilleté aux Noix.

Serves 6

12 sheets of filo pastry (about 225 g/8 oz)

125 ml/4 fl oz walnut oil

3 apples, peeled, cored and very thinly sliced
  (about 550 g/1¹/₄ lb)

60 g/2 oz walnut pieces

60 g/2 oz sugar

1–2 tablespoons Armagnac or Cognac

27–30 cm/11–12 in metal pie tin

1 Heat the oven to 190°C/375°F/Gas Mark 5. Unroll the filo pastry sheets flat on the work surface. Set the pie tin on top and trim the sheets to make rounds about 10 cm/4 in larger than the tin (don't worry if the dough is too narrow along two sides). Brush the tin with walnut oil and lay a sheet of dough in the bottom, draping excess dough over the sides. Brush lightly with oil and lay another sheet on top, at a 1 o'clock angle. Brush with oil, scatter with 4–5 apple slices and a few walnut pieces, and sprinkle with sugar and Armagnac or Cognac. Add another sheet at 2 o'clock. Continue brushing with oil and adding filling until all the filo is used, ending with a sheet of pastry. You'll need to work quickly as filo pastry dries out. If you have to pause, cover the unused sheets with a slightly dampened cloth.

2 Brush the edges of the pastry with a little more oil and twist and pleat them loosely over the galette to form a border about 5 cm/2 in wide. Brush the top of the galette with oil, sprinkle with sugar and bake in the oven for 30–40 minutes until crisp and golden brown. Serve it lukewarm.

Getting Ahead: Shape the galette up to 8 hours ahead and keep it tightly wrapped in the refrigerator, or freeze it for up to a month. I like to bake it just before serving, but it is still pretty good the following day.

On the Side: A glistening scoop of vanilla ice cream.

In the Glass: Look for one of those dark, intense fruit liqueurs such as wild raspberry, cassis (blackcurrant), or myrtille (bilberry). Or go for the gold with a straight shot of Armagnac.

Forget the chocolate truffles, it is crisp little cookies and petits fours that are my weakness. Acceptable ones are available ready made, but nothing can match the fragrant appeal of a personally styled treat that has been made at home. Texture is important, and so is shape – a cookie is all the more tempting when curved like a crescent moon.

Pistachio Crisps

(Makes 2 dozen 7.5 cm/3 in crisps)

When serving these crisps on their own, you may want to curl them over a rolling pin into a pretty tile shape. Or, for a spectacular dessert, leave the crisps flat and stack them in layers, sandwiching them with berries and whipped cream or ice cream. If your pistachios are salted, you will need to soak them in warm water for 15 minutes, then drain and dry them on paper towels.

125 g/4¹/₂ oz shelled pistachios
150 g/5¹/₂ oz sugar
75 g/2¹/₂ oz unbleached plain white flour
90 g/3 oz butter
75 ml/2¹/₂ oz light corn syrup

food processor

Toast the pistachios (page 166). Leave the oven on.

Let the pistachios cool, then put them with the sugar in the food processor. Finely grind them, using the pulse button, and put them in a bowl. Stir in the flour. Cut the butter in pieces and combine it in a bowl with the corn syrup. Set the bowl in a warm water bath and stir until the butter is melted. Pour the warm butter mixture into the pistachios and flour, and stir until mixed. Chill the mixture until stiff, about 15 minutes. Line a baking sheet with non-stick baking paper.

Bake a test crisp: roll a teaspoonful of mixture into a ball with your hands and set it on the baking sheet. Bake in the oven until melted and golden brown, 6–8 minutes. Let the crisp for cool 1–2 minutes until it is no longer very soft, then transfer it to a rack to cool completely. It should be crisp and very thin. If too thick, stir another tablespoon of melted butter into the batter.

Run the baking sheet under cold water to cool it. Line it again with paper and continue baking the crisps in the same way, 4–6 at a time. Store them in an airtight container for up to a week. If they lose crispness, warm them for a few minutes in a low oven.

Czech Almond Crescents

(Makes 50–60 crescents)

Just occasionally, a treat is worth a special effort. These meltingly rich cookies, Czech *rohlicky*, were brought one Christmas by my cousin Caroline, whose parents came from Prague. They can be mixed quickly in a food processor but they take a bit of time to shape ('Have a *slivovitz* plum brandy to speed the process,' says Caroline). *Rohlicky* mature if made a week or more ahead and stored in an airtight container.

90 g/3 oz whole unblanched almonds
90 g/3 oz granulated sugar
250 g/9 oz unbleached plain white flour
170 g/6 oz butter
1 vanilla pod
140 g/5 oz icing sugar, more if needed

food processor

Grind the almonds with the sugar in the processor until very fine, about 30 seconds. Add the flour and work for a few seconds until mixed. Add the butter, cut in small pieces, and pulse until mixed and the dough forms large sticky crumbs, about 1 minute. Turn it on to a floured board and knead with the heel of your hand until smooth, 1–2 minutes.

Line a baking sheet with non-stick baking paper. Scoop a small walnut-sized piece of dough and roll into a ball. Roll the dough into a cylinder and set it on the baking sheet, curving it to a gentle crescent. Repeat with the remaining dough. Chill until firm, about 30 minutes.

Heat the oven to 150°C/300°F/Gas Mark 2. Bake in the oven until firm and lightly browned, 18–20 minutes.

For vanilla sugar, slit open the vanilla pod and scrape the seeds into the icing sugar. Sift on to a tray. When the crescents are done, let them cool slightly then transfer a few at a time to the sugar. Toss with two forks until coated. Transfer to another sheet of paper and cool completely. Dust them with more icing sugar.

TIPS FOR DRESSING UP COOKIES

Good packaged cookies can be given a homemade touch with the following quick ideas:

Make a citrus glaze: Sift 100 g/3½ oz icing sugar into a bowl. Stir in 3–4 tablespoons of lemon or orange juice, enough to make a soft, pourable glaze. Lay the cookies on a sheet of parchment paper and then drizzle the glaze over them in a decorative pattern with a spoon or fork.

Make a chocolate glaze by finely chopping 90 g/3 oz semi-sweet chocolate. Bring 60 ml/2 fl oz cream to the boil in a small saucepan, and pour over the chocolate. Stir with a whisk until the chocolate is completely melted and the glaze is smooth. Drizzle over the cookies.

For pretty half-moons or triangles of chocolate, dip round or square cookies halfway in melted chocolate, allowing the excess to drip back into the bowl. If you like, sprinkle finely chopped nuts over the chocolate before it has set. Let the cookies dry on parchment paper.

Basic Recipes and Techniques

Bouquet garni: A bundle of aromatic herbs used for flavouring braises, râgouts and sauces. It should include 2–3 thyme sprigs, 1–2 bay leaves and several sprigs of parsley, tied together with string. Green leek and celery tops can also be included.

Brown stock: (Makes 2.5 litres/4^{1}/$_{2}$ pints) Brown stock is used for brown sauces, stews and braises based on red meats and game.

Roast 2.25 kg/5 lb veal bones (use half veal bones and half beef bones, if you like) in a very hot oven for 20 minutes. Add 2 quartered onions and continue roasting until very brown, almost scorched, about 30 minutes longer. Transfer the bones and vegetables to a stock pot, discarding any fat. Add a bouquet garni, along with 1 teaspoon whole peppercorns, 1 tablespoon tomato purée and about 5 litres/8^{3}/$_{4}$ pints water. Bring slowly to the boil, then simmer the stock, uncovered, for 4–5 hours, skimming occasionally. Strain, taste and, if the flavour is not concentrated, boil the stock until well reduced. Chill it and skim off any fat before using. Stock can be refrigerated for up to three days, or frozen. Freeze it in small, convenient containers.

Chicken stock: (Makes about 2.5 litres/4^{1}/$_{2}$ pints) This versatile stock can be used for soups and a variety of stews and sauces, as well as poultry dishes. Duck and other poultry can be substituted for the chicken.

In a large pan combine 1.35 kg/3 lb chicken backs, necks and bones, 1 quartered onion, 1 quartered carrot, 1 celery stick cut into pieces, a bouquet garni, 1 teaspoon peppercorns and about 4 litres/7 pints water. Bring the stock slowly to a boil, skimming often. Simmer uncovered, skimming occasionally, for 2–3 hours. Strain, taste and, if the stock is not concentrated, boil it until well reduced. Refrigerate and, before using, skim any solidified fat from its surface. Stock can be kept for up to three days in the refrigerator, or frozen.

Fish stock: (Makes about 1 litre/1^{3}/$_{4}$ pints) To maintain the fresh taste of fish, this is the only stock that is cooked fast and for only 20 minutes. Use it for fish stews and sauces.

Break 675 g/1^{1}/$_{2}$ lb fish bones into pieces and wash them thoroughly. In a pan, cook 1 sliced onion in 15 g/^{1}/$_{2}$ oz butter until soft but not brown. Add the fish bones, 1 litre/1^{3}/$_{4}$ pints water, a bouquet garni, 10 peppercorns and 250 ml/8 fl oz dry white wine. Bring to a boil and simmer, for 20 minutes, skimming often. Strain and cool.

Shortcrust pastry: As its name implies, shortcrust is a light dough that is more crumbling than pie pastry. For ingredient quantities, see individual recipes.

Sift the flour with the salt into a bowl. Add the butter and shortening or lard and cut them into small pieces with a pastry cutter or two table knives, using one in each hand. Rub with your fingertips until the mixture forms fine crumbs, lifting and crumbling to help aerate it. Make a well in the centre and add the water. Stir quickly to form crumbs. If dry, mix in 1–2 tablespoons more water. Press the dough together with your fingers. It should be soft but not sticky. Work it lightly with your hand for a few seconds to form a rough ball. Wrap the dough in plastic wrap and chill until firm, about 30 minutes.

Sweet shortcrust pastry: The European style of sweet pie pastry, laden with sugar and egg yolks, is easy to make in a processor or electric mixer. For measurements, see individual recipes.

Using a food processor: put the sugar, egg yolks, vanilla and butter in a food processor and work until smooth, about 30 seconds. Add the flour and salt and pulse briefly, just until the mixture starts to bind into coarse crumbs, 30–40 seconds.

Using a mixer: cream the butter with the whisk and beat in the sugar until light and fluffy, 2–3 minutes. Beat in the egg yolks. Turn off the machine, add the flour and mix it with the speed at low until coarse crumbs form. Tip the crumbs on to a lightly floured work surface and press them into a ball with your hands.

Knead the dough: with the heel of your hand, push it away from you, then gather it up with a pastry scraper or metal spatula. Repeat the action 4–5 times. You'll find the dough loses its rough texture and becomes very smooth and pliable; if it seems sticky, work in 1–2 tablespoons more flour. Wrap the dough in plastic wrap and chill until firm, about 30 minutes.

To line a tart tin: If possible use a tart tin with a removable base so the shell can be removed easily. Brush the tin with butter. Roll out the dough to a round of 6 mm/^{1}/$_4$ in thickness, about 5 cm/2 in larger than the diameter of the tin. Wrap the dough around the rolling pin, lift it over the tin and unroll it. Let the dough rest loosely over the edge of the tin, overlapping it slightly inside. Lift the edges of dough and press it well into the bottom corners. Run the rolling pin over the top of the tin to cut off excess dough.

With your forefinger and thumb, press the dough evenly up the sides from the bottom to increase the height of the edge. Neaten the edge with your finger and thumb, and flute it if you are making a sweet tart. Prick the base of the pastry case so that the dough cooks evenly. Chill thoroughly before baking.

To bake a pastry case blind (empty): A shell is baked blind if the filling is not to be cooked in the case, or if the filling is especially moist and might make the pastry soggy during baking. The dried beans or rice for blind baking can be kept and re-used.

Heat the oven to 200°C/400°F/Gas Mark 6. Crumple a round of foil or nonstick baking paper and line the chilled pastry case, pressing the paper into the corners. Fill with dried beans or rice. Bake the pastry in the oven for 15 minutes or until the edges are set and lightly browned. Remove the paper and beans or rice and bake until the base is firm and dry, for 4–5 minutes if the tart is to be baked again with the filling, or until well browned, 8–10 minutes, to bake the shell completely.

Toasting and peeling hazelnuts: Heat the oven to 180°/350°F/Gas Mark 4. Spread the nuts in a single layer on a shallow tin or baking sheet with edges and toast them in the oven until browned, 12–15 minutes. Let them cool slightly and, if not already peeled, rub them with a rough cloth to remove the skins.

Toasting nuts: Heat the oven to 180°C/350°F/Gas Mark 4. Spread the nuts on a baking sheet and bake until crisp, stirring occasionally so they toast evenly, 5–8 minutes.

Tomatoes, to peel, seed and chop: Pour boiling water over the tomatoes and leave for 10 seconds or until the skin starts to peel. Drain the tomatoes and peel them. Halve them crosswise and squeeze to remove the seeds; then chop them, discarding the cores. The seeds can be sieved to extract the juice.

Trussing with string: This more casual approach to trussing a whole bird does not involve a trussing needle. It's a good idea to remove the wishbone first, to make carving easier. Lift the neck skin and, with a small sharp knife, outline the wishbone and cut it free from the breastbone. Tuck the neck skin and wings under the bird. Set it on its back. Tie a long string around the tail and knot it over the leg joints, tying a double knot. Take the strings back along the sides of the body, passing them between the legs and the breast. Flip the bird over on to its breast and loop the strings under each wing pinion. Tie the strings tightly, again with a double knot, and turn the bird over on its back. You'll see that legs and wings are held firmly to the body and the bird sits flat on the board.

Veal stock: Veal stock is used for lighter sauces to serve with veal, pork and poultry.

Proceed as for brown stock, using only veal bones, but do not brown the bones and vegetables, and omit the tomato purée. Blanch the bones, then continue as for brown stock.

Vegetable stock: (Makes about 1.5 litres/2^{1}/$_2$ pints) A mild, fresh-tasting stock that can be substituted for veal or chicken.

In a large saucepan combine: 3 onions, diced; 3 carrots, diced; 3 celery sticks, diced; and 2 garlic cloves (optional). Add 2 litres/3^{1}/$_2$ pints water, a bouquet garni and 10 peppercorns. Bring slowly to a boil, and simmer the stock, uncovered, for 1 hour, skimming occasionally. Remove the stock from the heat and strain. Let cool, then cover and keep in the refrigerator. If frozen, this type of stock tends to be tasteless.

Index